DAWN 2000:

ches To

*The personal story of the DAWN
strategy for world evangelization*

JIM MONTGOMERY

William Carey Library

Pasadena, California

Published by
William Carey Library
P.O. Box 40129
Pasadena, California 91114
(818) 798-0819

Printed in the United States of America

———————————————————————————

ISBN 0-87808-220-4

L.C.#89-061042

Cover design by Jim Mills

To Lyn

It was our farewell party from Overseas Crusades and Ed Murphy was saying a few kind words about the life and times of Jim Montgomery.

Next, he started in on my wife, Lyn. I noticed it was taking a lot longer to extol her virtues. I thought he was getting carried away on the subject of how much Lyn had contributed to my ministry.

Finally, he got to the bottom line: "In fact, Jim would have been nothing at all without Lyn," he said.

"Don't pour it on *too* thick, Ed," I wanted to say out loud.

It would have gotten a laugh, I suppose. But it also would have detracted from the truth.

I have written other books, and perhaps will publish again. But this book is more than just my project for 1988. More than anything, it is a life lived — a life that "would have been nothing at all without Lyn."

Thanks, Ed, for pointing out the truth for all the world to know.

Jim Montgomery
March 7, 1989

"... waiting for *and hastening*
the coming of the day of God...."

2 Peter 3:12

Contents

Foreword

What kind of a person could possibly write a book on 7 million churches which have not yet been planted?

What kind of a person could even think of such a thing?

Jim Montgomery is that person. This book, the first definitive treatment of the DAWN (Discipling a Whole Nation) movement, will certainly take its place as one of the premier missiological works of the closing years of the 20th Century. It is a book which has all the marks of a classic even before it gets to the bookstore shelves.

Only an individual with an extraordinary gift of faith could look out on a troubled and confusing world and see the power of God moving so strongly that there would be one church within easy access of every 400 to 1,000 persons on earth by the end of the century. My personal association with Jim Montgomery spans more than two decades. Knowing him is knowing a man of God who not only accurately perceives God's long-range purposes, but has the courage to step out and take the risks often necessary to serve him as those purposes take shape.

This book is not only the story of DAWN, but it is the warm and moving story of Jim and Lyn Montgomery as they have given their bodies as a living sacrifice for the completion of the Great Commission. Nothing exemplifies their faith and courage more than the bold step they took in mid-career to leave a comfortable position in an established mission agency to pioneer Dawn Ministries, fully expecting to lose their home, their car, their regular income and who knows what else. And nothing could highlight God's faithfulness more than his constant, loving provision of their needs ever since.

I have been quoted as affirming that I believe DAWN to be the most effective delivery system in existence today for allowing church growth principles to be applied to the grass roots. Let me elaborate on this.

Throughout Christian history, over 700 plans have been devised for global evangelization, usually within one generation. Most of these plans have fizzled. DAWN is one of those plans, but it is different from the others. Not that I would be so bold as to predict that by AD 2000 the world will be evangelized largely because of the DAWN movement. But I will predict that if the principles in *DAWN 2000: 7 Million Churches To Go* are understood and implemented in country after country, the world will be much closer to being evangelized than it ever has been before.

Historically, DAWN is the linear successor of the Vergil Gerber church growth workshops conducted throughout the world during the 1970s. In over 50 countries Vergil Gerber taught church growth principles to pastors, encouraged them to set faith goals for growth, and motivated them to pay the price to accomplish the goals. As a result the growth rate of many churches and denominations from Argentina to Zambia dramatically increased. Gerber's "manual" was translated into over 40 languages and continues to exert a powerful influence among church leaders.

DAWN has picked up where Gerber left off. Using more advanced church growth technology, more extensive research, a broader base of coordination, a longer term and more demanding process, and an extensive accountability system, Jim Montgomery represents a second generation which has added many improvements to Vergil Gerber's basics. Goal setting, for example, remains a key internal dynamic of DAWN.

Theologically DAWN is effective because it adheres to

the biblical view of evangelism as not just establishing a Christian presence, nor simply proclaiming the gospel message, but actually "making disciples" (Mt. 28:19). Disciples are individuals who have faith in Jesus Christ as Savior and Lord and who become responsible church members. Research has shown that evangelistic efforts which are built on this theological base are more effective in winning people to Christ. Unfortunately only 3 percent of the over 700 global plans have declared that making disciples was their goal. No wonder so many have fizzled.

Ecclesiastically DAWN is strong because it recognizes and respects the existing structures of churches, denominations, and parachurch organizations in a given country. Rather than bypassing these structures or offering to modify them, DAWN simply catalyzes them in an effort to release the latent spiritual power which most of them already possess. Rather than being a threat to Christian leaders, DAWN is more readily seen as a resource to help them accomplish their evangelistic task more effectively.

These are only a few of the reasons why I believe that *DAWN 2000: 7 Million Churches To Go* is one of those unusual books which is destined to make a significant, measurable impact on the evangelization of the world.

C. Peter Wagner
Fuller Seminary School of World Mission
Pasadena, California

Part One

What DAWN Is

Chapter 1

No Dove on My Shoulder

For 27 years, Overseas Crusades had been "my" mission. With O.C., my wife Lyn and I had spent four years in Taiwan, 13 in the Philippines, a short stint in Guatemala and ten years at the home office near San Jose, California, in various leadership positions.

In 1958, we had boarded a plane for Taiwan with Sheryl, our only child. It was her first birthday. Cindy was born a few months later in Taiwan. Len was three months old when we returned to the Philippines in 1965.

Founded by the beloved Dick Hillis in 1952, Overseas Crusades was, in my opinion, the best and most exciting society in missions. I loved it, believed in it, felt ownership of its purposes. I also felt it had vast, untapped potential in the whole arena of world evangelization. I felt an optimum strategy for completing the Great Commission could be built on its philosophy of ministry.

Strange and out of place

Then why did I feel, in the summer of 1984, strange and

out of place? It happened during the training and retraining program for prospective missionaries, new missionaries and missionaries on furlough. We were holding the session I loved most when the furloughed missionaries were turned loose on the Executive Leadership Team. They could ask any question they wanted on any topic. How I relished those encounters!

That day, however, I said almost not a word. Others were answering the questions I had loved responding to. It began to dawn on me that the mission now belonged to others. I felt the load of responsibility I had willingly carried for the mission for more than a quarter century lifting. I was in great turmoil.

Two days later on a Sunday afternoon, I went for a walk toward the hills near our home on the east side of San Jose. As I had done in the past during troubled times, I began to think of the glories of heaven when all stress and uncertainty would be over. But my thoughts were interrupted.

"Actually, heaven will be a lousy place, Lord," I found myself praying, "if I go there — in not too many years at most — without having accomplished your will for me on earth. I beg you to show me your will now. I *must* know your will."

In that troubled frame of mind, I trespassed into an old apricot orchard on a hillside from where I could almost see the neighborhood where I had been born and reared more than a half century before. I prayed, meditated, opened my heart to the Lord.

Could I just cruise along in the comfort and security of O.C. until I could collect my pension in a few years? Could I, at age 55, step out on my own and begin all over again? A flock of doves flew past. I hoped one of them would alight on my shoulder and give me a sign of what I ought to do.

None did, and I ultimately trudged home without an answer. "I'm a morning person anyway, Lord. Perhaps you want to speak to me tomorrow when I get up to read your Word," I prayed.

The father I never knew

The next morning, chapter 17 of John "happened" to be next up in my reading. Let me explain the quotes.

I'm told that my father, James H. Montgomery, Sr., was a godly man who loved the Lord and loved his Word. He became ill with tuberculosis when I was two and spent the next five years in a T.B. sanitarium in the Veterans Hospital at Livermore, California. My sisters, Lucille and Marjorie, and I were allowed to see him only rarely lest we contract the dread disease that at that time had no cure.

He died in 1937 without my ever really knowing him, though perhaps he lives on in me through his prayers. That hadn't occurred to me until Lucille made mention of it a few years ago.

"I believe that all that my brother has accomplished for the Lord is the result of the prayers of my father," she told a group of ladies in a home meeting.

It made sense. After all, what does a godly young man in his early thirties do day after day for five years in a hospital bed? Surely he prays for, among others, his infant and only son.

I can't tell you what a source of comfort and strength that thought has been to me in recent years. I still get choked up when I relate this story.

The only tangible connection I have with this godly man is a penciled manuscript he wrote while in the hospital. As he pored over the Word, he came to the conclusion that one particular chapter in the New Testament was the key to the whole of scripture. The manuscript is the detailed study of how each verse of this chapter relates to a particular section of the Bible.

So when I say that I "happened" to be reading that morning from John 17, you can guess what chapter it was my father had concluded was the key to all scripture. It was this same passage — the prayer of our Lord before he went to be with the Father.

"Father, the hour has come," I read from John 17:1. But

5

that was as far as I got. I knew instantly and without a doubt what the rest of the sentence was for me that morning. The hour had come for me to leave O.C. and develop the dream and vision the Lord had laid on my heart. It was time to start a new mission agency.

In the days and weeks that were to follow, other scriptures, various circumstances, the enthusiastic acceptance of my wife and children and the counsel of trusted elders in my life all confirmed this call.

Doubting Thomas

I immediately assumed, by the way, this would mean losing the house and car and living hand to mouth for a few years. People sometimes call me a man of faith and vision. The reality is I identify primarily with the Apostle Thomas, i.e., "doubting" Thomas. I personally don't see him so much a doubter as simply having a negative personality.

Think about the time, for instance, when all others were begging the Lord to stay away from Jerusalem since people there wanted to kill him. Thomas is the one, however, who stood up and said, "Let us also go, *that we may die with him.*" He was eager to do what was right, but expected the worst to happen. To me, that's real courage.

And that's how I felt about my financial prospects in following the leading of the Lord to start a new mission agency. I knew I had to step out by faith and start over, but I expected to lose everything in the process.

The one thing I wasn't ready to let go of, however, was my son Len's education. By scraping together every possible nickel, he had been able to complete one year at Biola University. What would happen now that all my financial resources were going up in smoke?

Instead of beating me over the head with my lack of faith, the Lord sent "Stretch" and Hilda Cayward to our door one night. Early in the conversation, they brought up

Len's schooling. "How are you going to pay for it?" they asked.

Len had a couple of small scholarships, but the rest would be up to the Lord.

"We'll pay for it," they said. And they did, for the next two years. They hadn't even known we were starting a new mission agency!

Furthermore, four years have passed since we left O.C. and we have yet to have a financial crisis either personally or in the mission. But I'm still mentally prepared for our first real crunch when it comes!

Eight years of preparation

Dawn Ministries is actually the fulfillment of an insight the Lord had given eight years previously. On a plane to Atlanta, the Lord spoke clearly about starting what I began calling an "International Ministries Team." Such a team — within O.C., I assumed — would carry out the vision of what is now Dawn Ministries.

Eight years would pass serving under O.C. presidents Luis Palau and Clyde Cook as well as a year under acting president Paul Yaggy and the first few months of the Larry Keyes administration. I had so much to learn, and those years spent facing every possible situation that might come up in a mission agency were necessary preparation for what would come. I never expected, however, that the vision the Lord had given me would be carried out in any structure other than O.C.

But now the hour had come for me to finish the work the Lord had given me. The leading was so clear and so strong that Lyn and I have never looked back. It was time to start what would become Dawn Ministries.

A completely different society

But just what was it Dawn Ministries was called to do?

It would be a completely different type of society, built

7

on the realities of missions as we approach the last decade of this millennium. Some of the realities that occurred to me included these:

• We have seen tremendously increased costs for sending career missionaries overseas, perhaps averaging around $50,000 a year to place, keep and provide home office backup for a missionary family on the field. When it is remembered that it takes up to two years to raise support, two to four years on the field for language learning and acculturation, that this is followed by a year of furlough after which many missionaries do not return, the true cost of missions can be seen in better perspective.

• Traditional Western missionaries as such are now excluded from 65 percent of the world's population. This is expected to go up to 83 percent by the end of the century. Even if we were financially able to send thousands of traditional missionaries to the unreached peoples of China, India and the Muslim world, for example, no visas would be extended to most of these volunteers. It's also true that even where we can get in with a visa we are not necessarily welcomed by the national Church!

• After 200 years of the modern missionary effort, the Church is now well established in almost every country in the world. There are now strong, godly and experienced national leaders capable of completing the task so sacrificially begun by foreigners.

• Today's world includes more winnable people than ever. Hosea's comment that "in their misery they will earnestly seek me" (5:15) surely would be true not only for the nation of Israel but all nations of the earth. As traumatic conditions only get more severe around the world, there are more and more people looking for better answers. One result is the reality of a greater potential harvest than ever being reported in nation after nation.

• Since the Lausanne Congress in 1974, there has been a mounting concern for thousands of still unreached peoples of the world along with a growing excitement about targeting the year 2000 for completing the task of evangelizing them.

Added to this is the burgeoning of missionary interest among Third World Churches.

To say the new Dawn Ministries agency would take these realities into consideration in developing its strategy is not to say, of course, that traditional missionaries are obsolete or that there are not other alternatives to carrying out the Great Commission. God will guide the leaders of every structure in the way he wants it to go, and I will be a fervent supporter of each.

But here is the way the Lord had been leading us to face these realities:

• We would develop a small team of experienced missionaries capable of motivating and training the top level of leaders in a country to organize a nationwide project that would lead most directly to the discipling of that country and all the peoples within it. Such a strategy would be called DAWN — Discipling A Whole Nation.

• These missionaries would not be sent to reside in any nation overseas. Rather, they would communicate the vision of the DAWN strategy through various publications, seminars and travels throughout the world.

• Their primary task would be to locate and equip what we would call the "John Knoxer" of a nation. That is, such a person would have the same burden as the intrepid reformer whose heart's cry was "Give me Scotland or I die." The John Knoxer would of necessity also have the abilities to mobilize the Church of a nation for a DAWN-type project.

• Dawn Ministries would work towards the goal of being in contact with such a leader in every nation of the world by 1995 so that there could be a DAWN project in operation for every country by AD 2000. (In some cases, it would be impossible for such a person actually to live within his country. Creative ways would need to be found to develop a DAWN project in such situations.)

• Dawn missionaries, then, would serve in two basic capacities: 1) They would communicate the vision of DAWN. 2) They would serve as consultants and helpers to the John Knoxers who desired to develop DAWN projects.

Using this approach, it would then be possible for a small band of individuals at a very low total cost to help mobilize the whole body of Christ in whole countries and ultimately in the whole world to a much greater effort in completing the Great Commission.

The bottom line is that Dawn Ministries, the organization, would spread the vision of DAWN, the strategy. It would attempt to fan the flames of a movement for world evangelization that seemed to be catching on very rapidly in country after country around the world.

But what is DAWN, the strategy? Where did it come from? Who is behind it? How does it work? Can it truly help speed world evangelization? What has it got to do with 7 million more churches?

That's what this book is all about.

Chapter 2

The DAWN Strategy

DAWN is an acronym flowing from Matthew 28:19 and 20 that stands for "Disciple A Whole Nation." It is the name of a strategy for world evangelization that is gaining acceptance around the world by many leaders.

To tell the truth, I've been somewhat flabbergasted at the speed with which the DAWN idea has spread and the endorsements it has received.

"DAWN is the best strategy yet developed for world evangelization," says C. Peter Wagner of the Fuller School of World Mission. "It is the best program I know of for bringing church growth to the grass-roots level on an international basis."

"DAWN is the most basic strategy of all strategies," says Ralph Winter of the U.S. Center for World Mission. "There are other things that need to be done besides DAWN, but that is the starting place for completing the Great Commission."

"DAWN is a mature reaction to the Great Commission," says Bruno Frigoli, an Argentine missionary on the Lausanne Committee who is now serving in Peru.

"DAWN is an idea whose time has come, there is no question about that," says Bernard Camper of MARC Canada. "It is one of the great movements God has raised up in the last half of the 20th century for the completion of the Great Commission."

"DAWN is a one-word summary of the Great Commission," says a Methodist Church leader in Gweru, Zimbabwe. "Jesus told his followers to make disciples of all nations. DAWN is the essence of our Lord's command . . . and it encourages us to get on with the job in Zimbabwe."

"DAWN is probably one of the most revolutionary principles of evangelism to be pressed upon Christ's Church by the Holy Spirit in our generation," writes Ed Murphy of Overseas Crusades.

"DAWN is exactly the program we need in our country right now," says leader after leader around the world.

When I contemplate how the whole DAWN idea developed, how God's chosen leaders around the world respond to it and what it has actually accomplished so far, I am forced to the conclusion that it comes from the heart of God. It is not an ivory tower Western idea, nor an idea from the mind of any one man. It seems to be one of the strategies the Lord is giving his Church as we approach the close of this age.

The DAWN strategy

DAWN aims at mobilizing the whole body of Christ in whole countries in a determined effort to complete the Great Commission in that country by working toward the goal of providing an evangelical congregation for every village and neighborhood of every class, kind and condition of people in the whole country.

It is concerned that Jesus Christ become incarnate in all his beauty, compassion, power and message in the midst of every small group of people — 400 or so to 1,000 or more in number — in a whole country including all its people groups.

When this is accomplished, it is *not* assumed the Great

Commission for a country has been completed, but that the last practical and measurable goal has been reached toward making a disciple of that country and all the "nations" within it.

With a witnessing congregation in every small community of people, it is now possible to communicate the gospel in the most direct, contextualized and productive way to every person in that land.

Every person now has a reasonable opportunity to make an informed, intelligent decision for or against Jesus Christ.

Everyone now has a church within easy access both in a practical as well as cultural sense where he or she can attend and be further trained in discipleship should he or she become a believer.

The penultimate step for making a disciple of every "nation" in a country has been reached.

In a nutshell, that is what DAWN is all about. When this happens in *every* country in the world, we can almost hear the trumpet sound. The primary task the Lord gave his Church is close to completion and the Lord can soon return for his bride.

The idea germinates

This DAWN idea, of course, does not originate with me or any one person. Even the acronym — to give credit where it is due — was first suggested by Donald McGavran, the missiologist of the century from whose mind and heart have come so many other fertile ideas. He applied it to the strategy and project that was being developed in the Philippines in the early 1970s.

Though I was involved in developing that strategy, there were others who were writing about and experimenting with the idea that formed its core: the multiplication of local churches until a city, a region, a people, a country, even the whole world was filled with them.

Reporting on a conference of three missiologists and three missionaries in 1966, for example, Ed Dayton,

currently a Vice President of World Vision and Chairman
of the Strategy Working Group of the Lausanne Committee,
wrote:

> In order to make progress toward world evangel-
> ization, we need a goal for world evangelization.
> . . . We therefore selected as our working goal . . .
> that "There should be ten witnessing Christians
> in every town of more than 500 people in the
> world."[1]

In his book, *Breaking the Stained Glass Barrier*, David
Womack, an Assemblies of God missionary, wrote that
"There is only one way the Great Commission can be fulfilled, and that is by establishing gospel-preaching congregations in every community on the face of the earth."[2]

Roger Greenway, a specialist in reaching cities, says in
Discipling the City that "the church's evangelistic task . . .
demands that every barrio, apartment building, and
neighborhood have a church faithful to God's word established in it."[3]

Ralph Winter, while emphasizing the "greater
urgency" of planting the first congregation in thousands of
still unreached people groups, wrote in a letter to me that
"it seems to me that we should say 'a church for every
people group in the world and at least one for every 1,000
within those groups.'"[4]

Donald McGavran has possibly expressed the case most
clearly when he stated that:

> The goal of the Great Commission . . . is the
> establishment of a cell (church) of committed
> Christians in every community, every neighbor-
> hood, every class and condition of people, where
> everyone can hear and see demonstrated the
> gospel from his own intimates, in his tongue, and
> has a reasonable opportunity to become a disciple
> of Jesus Christ.[5]

In another place he wrote "This truth . . . means first

14

that giving opportunity to all men to appropriate salvation can truly be done by establishing millions of congregations of practicing Christians, ideally one in every small community of men and women."[6]

J. Robertson McQuilkin wrote along the same lines:

> His command was to disciple the nations (Mt. 28:18ff). What the world will look like when the Great Commission has been fully obeyed and God's purposes for the era of the Church have been accomplished, we do not know. However, in the light of the command, the Church must assume that it has not completed Christ's purposes until every person has had an opportunity to hear with understanding the gospel and until disciples have been made, establishing a community of God's people, the congregation, in each locality.[7]

Some DAWN prototypes

So as the years rolled by in developing the DAWN strategy, I found I was not alone in coming to the conclusion that filling the earth with congregations of the incarnate Christ was the most direct approach to world evangelization. Furthermore, I discovered at least one prototype program of church multiplication whose goal was the saturating of a whole country with local, evangelical congregations.

This was the work of Hugh Linton in Korea. Back in 1966, he and his co-workers made a careful survey of their area and developed a seven-year plan to put a congregation in "each village of more than 100 houses four kilometers distance from the nearest evangelical church."[8]

I recently came across another example of this kind of thinking when I was in South Africa. William Crew of the Hatfield Christian Church was telling me about their program that I began calling the Three P Movement, for their rallying cry was to "Plant the Presence of Christ in every Place in Southern Africa."[9]

Their statistics indicated this was much more than just a slogan. In the 33-month period from mid-1984 to April 1987, they saw their flock increase from 22 congregations to 154! This represents an AAGR (Average Annual Growth Rate) of 90 percent! The mother church had a membership of about 4,500, and, with 70 percent of their daughter churches reporting, they counted a total average attendance of 42,000.

While talking with me, Crew made the comment that our presentation of the DAWN strategy in one of our seminars in Johannesburg was an "incredible affirmation of what we are doing." I responded that this worked the other way around as well. What the Lord had led *them* to do was another "incredible affirmation" that the whole idea was from the Lord.

The first DAWN project

Since then I have come across a number of similar plans on local or district levels that aim at a church within walking distance of every person or some such equivalent.

But the first actual project that spawned the DAWN movement began in the Philippines in 1974 when about 75 church and mission leaders committed themselves to work toward the goal of a church in every barrio by AD 2000. This would mean growing from about 5,000 churches to 50,000 in 26 years.

As I write this, I've just returned from the third DAWN Congress held in the Philippines, this one the week of October 10-14, 1988. Jun Vencer, Chairman of the Philippine Council of Evangelical Churches that is sponsoring what has become known as DAWN 2000, was able to report that the Church is still on schedule for reaching this goal. It has more than doubled its church-planting rate of growth from 5 percent AAGR in the '60s to more than 11 percent for each succeeding year.

If the church continues to grow at this rate until AD 2000, and there is every reason to believe it will, it will not only exceed the goal of 50,000 churches but will have planted at least 36,000 more churches than it would have at the old rate and seen around 4 million more new converts become active members of those churches than would have.

The idea spreads

Hearing of this model, about 350 Guatemalan Church leaders in an Amanecer (Spanish for Dawn) Congress in 1984 committed themselves to the goal of seeing evangelicals become 50 percent of the population of their country by 1990. They would do this by doubling their 7,500 churches to 15,000. A recent report by Roy Wingerd, a researcher with Overseas Crusades, indicates that 15 denominations alone have projects under way that could result in this goal being reached.

Neighboring El Salvador in a congress in 1987 set their goals at 30 percent of the population by 1990, 50 percent by 1996 — their centennial year for protestant missions — and 75 percent by AD 2000! Again, they would work toward these goals through the multiplication of local churches.

In April 1985, several hundred leaders meeting in a congress in Zaire rallied around the goal of planting at least one church in each of 10,000 unchurched villages in the country in five years, and 5,000 additional churches in their cities. In 1988, about 2,000 churches were planted through just one project, and their goal for this same project in 1989 is an additional 5,000! Furthermore, they are making plans that would see about 70,000 new churches in all planted in the next five years!

In Indonesia, Chris Marantika has developed a program called "One, One, One." This stands for "*one* church in each *one* village in *one* generation." A plan developed on a very successful model sees this accomplished by AD 2015. It calls for starting tens of thousands of churches by men and women trained in 415 two-year seminaries being scattered

17

throughout the land. The program is now catching fire with denominations that seem poised to take up the challenge with Marantika.

Leaders in such countries as Japan, India, Ghana, New Zealand, Zimbabwe, Nigeria, Canada, Finland, Spain, South Africa, Bolivia and a growing number of other nations have either committed themselves to similar programs or are seriously considering them.

7 million churches to go

Our dream and goal in Dawn Ministries, an agency we believe God has raised up to fan the flames of this movement, is to see at least the beginning of DAWN projects in every nation in the world by 1995. If every country were working toward a goal that would see a congregation in existence in every small group of every class, kind and condition of people in that country, we would need to add about 7 million more churches by AD 2000. Added to the current number that could be as high as 3 million, we would have a total of 10 million or on average one for every 600 people in the world by the end of the century.

The task is monstrously more complicated than just the raw number, of course. And even the raw number is more symbolic than scientific. The actual number of new churches needed or that could in reality be planted might be closer to 5 million or 9 million, depending on definitions, vitality of existing churches and various cultural and societal conditions.

So let's not quibble over the number, at least not until you've read further into the book. The last thing we can afford is to use any more precious creative energy in pointless hassling over definitions and finite numbers. What evangelicals need is not further theological debate concerning the Great Commission but a strategy we can all agree on. Enough generations and centuries have passed with the Command only partially obeyed.

After you have finished this book, you can choose your own number, as well as the number you want to see your organization and the Church of your country work toward.

As for me, my hope for these first two chapters is that the reader has just enough information to be motivated sufficiently to go back with me to the beginnings of the DAWN idea, to see how and why it developed, how it leads to the goal of 7 million new churches, how reasonable the goal is and how we can work most directly at achieving it. I hope I have succeeded.

That's a lot of ground to cover, so let's go back and take it from the top.

Notes

1. Edward Dayton, "Disciplined Planning and Data Retrieval," in *God, Man and Church Growth*, ed. Tippett (Grand Rapids: Eerdmans, 1973), p. 147.
2. David Womack, *Breaking the Stained Glass Barrier*, (New York: Harper and Row, 1973), p. 88.
3. Roger Greenway, "Content and Context: The Whole Christ for the Whole City," in *Discipling the City*, ed. Greenway (Grand Rapids: Baker Book House, 1979), p. 104.
4. Personal letter on file.
5. Win Arn, "A Church Growth Look at Here's Life America," *Church Growth: America*, Jan./Feb. 1977, pp. 4-30.
6. Donald McGavran, "Imperialism and Church Multiplication," *Church Growth Bulletin*, May 1967, p. 225.
7. J. Robertson McQuilkin, *How Biblical is the Church Growth Movement?* (Chicago: Moody Press, 1973), p. 56.
8. Paul Rader, "Church Multiplying Missions in Korea," *Church Growth Bulletin*, July 1973, p. 343.
9. Jim Montgomery, "'3P Movement' Grows in Africa," *DAWN Report*, September 1987, p. 6.

Chapter 3

The Back Side of the Desert

Growing up under the 35-year ministry of Clarence Sands at First Baptist Church, San Jose, I absorbed the idea that coming to Christ, getting saved, was good for people. The engaging Sunday evening services as well as the twice-a-year evangelistic campaigns in the church produced a steady stream of converts. Drunks were cured, homes were healed, up-tight people entered the joy of the Lord.

If becoming a Christian were good for the few who happened to stumble into our church services, surely it must be good for everybody in town. In the country. In the world! At the time, nothing seemed more important in life than giving everyone an honest chance to take a close look at the living Christ and thereby be able to make an intelligent decision for or against him.

Thus did I begin to sense a calling to devote my life to the completion of the Great Commission: to "go into all the world" (Mk. 16:15) and "make disciples of all nations" (Mt. 28:19).

A whole college

My first "world" after that conviction came upon me

was San Jose State University. First Baptist was just two blocks from that campus of 7,000 students. I was president of the handful of college-age kids in church during my freshman year. What should we do?

We had in our hands a directory listing the name and address of every student. The only practical way to reach them all, it seemed, was by mail.

We wrote a letter, mimeographed it, hand signed it, enclosed a gospel tract and sent it off to all 7,000 kids.

I suppose it did some good. The growth rate of our college group was terrific. I have calculated that if the group had continued to grow at that same rate until the present, every man, woman and child in the world would now be attending Tri-C (Career, Campus, Christ) every Sunday night at First Baptist Church.

One thousand percent average annual growth rate (AAGR) is easier to achieve, however, when you start with ten and grow to 100 — as we did — than when you start with 10,000, say, and grow to 100,000, and keep growing at that pace year after year!

As I left the next year for what would become five years at Wheaton College, I was pleased with what had happened at San Jose State. But not satisfied. There were still almost 7,000 students on their way to hell. We had devised and carried out a simple strategy for reaching that "world," but had made only a tiny splash.

"Equip the saints"

At Wheaton, I eventually became involved in Young Life. Much of what I understand about incarnating Christ — though I don't remember that term being used — I learned from George Sheffer and my club work at St. Charles High School.

I really wasn't very good at this, and the high school was pretty much as pagan when I left as when I came. But I don't fault myself for not trying my best to reach this "world" that was available to me at Wheaton.

22

Another insight about world evangelization struck me when I took a Christian Education course my senior year under Lois LeBar. Her whole philosophy of ministry flowed out of Ephesians chapter four. (This was long before spiritual gifts and body life became generally popular in evangelical circles.)

Gifted people were given to the Church to equip the *saints* for the work of the ministry!

I had struggled with the logistics of getting enough full-time pastors, evangelists and missionaries to complete the task. But what if all the saints, all the laypeople, could be equipped for making disciples of all nations?

By various estimates, that now embraces between 300 and 400 million people! A third of a billion born by the Spirit of God and indwelt by his almighty power!

In this respect, Ralph Winter continues to remind us that while the task is four times as large now as it was in 1900, it is also true that we have 40 times the resources. That is, whereas there were about 10 million evangelicals in the world at that time, there are now perhaps 400 million!

Even as the superpowers have the nuclear weapons to kill everybody in the world many times over, so we have the resources a hundred times over to complete the task of world evangelization. If only we could fully equip all the saints in the world to work at it!

A whole valley

That thought rang in my ears as I returned to First Baptist in San Jose to become their first Minister of Christian Education after completing an M.A. in the subject at Wheaton grad school.

Now my "world" was all of Santa Clara Valley. I wanted to see First Baptist grow, but I wanted to see *every* church grow. I wanted to see the whole body of Christ in the whole county mobilized in the most direct attempt possible at discipling the whole county.

23

With permission from Pastor Sands, I got some area pastors together and formed what became known as the Greater San Jose Sunday School Association, which began holding annual conventions. If the way to complete the Great Commission were to equip the saints for the work of this ministry, then why not gather all the saints already somewhat involved and give them further inspiration and training?

Some good things came out of this convention movement that began in 1957. The early years were so successful that Clate Risley brought the National Convention to San Jose in 1959. In the years that followed, attendance at the local conventions reached 5,000 and more. In the 31 years of conventions, tens of thousands have been further "equipped for the ministry."

Furthermore, at least some churches grew. Marvin Rickard of the Los Gatos Christian Church, for example, credits some things he learned from Henrietta Mears in one of those early conventions for providing the foundation for the growth of his church. And what growth it was! From 67 members up to around five thousand with five or six daughter churches also up in the thousands.

But there was the now familiar gnawing reality as well. When I left for the mission field in 1958, there were still hundreds of thousands in the San Jose area that were no closer to coming to Christ than when we began. In fact, research done in 1985 indicated that on a given Sunday morning only 6.8 percent of all people in Santa Clara County could be found in a protestant church of any kind. After 30 years of the convention movement that was designed to equip the saints of Santa Clara Valley for evangelizing that Valley, there were still 1.3 million residents outside the body of Christ.

A whole country

Next came a four-year stint in Taiwan. My wife Lyn and I — now with one-year-old Sheryl — joined Overseas

24

Crusades because they, too, had a commitment to Ephesians 4. They wanted to mobilize and equip the whole body of Christ in whole countries for the discipling of those whole countries.

Instead of a whole school or whole valley, there was now a whole nation to be concerned with. Lyn and I entered missions as teachers of missionary kids, so I was not directly involved in the strategy for the discipling of Taiwan. But I did follow the process closely.

Under the leadership of Dick Hillis, the O.C. team set out to reach every one of 6,000 villages in the country. One thousand of them they sublet to another organization. For the remainder, they began a systematic process of evangelizing in every village.

The strategy was to go to a village where there was a church, train the pastor and lay leaders and take them out with a gospel truck to surrounding villages. With a sound system hooked up to the truck, they preached the gospel, counseled inquirers and invited people to sign up for a free Bible correspondence course.

It took ten years, but they completed the task. Some very good things came out of this strategy as well. Thousands of lay Christians were trained and put to work. Several hundred thousand people signed up for the Bible correspondence course. The Church of Taiwan doubled, though it would be difficult to say just how much of this growth came as a direct result of this project.

When Lyn and I left Taiwan after four years, however, I had to repeat to myself the familiar litany. A heroic effort using a soundly biblical approach to reach a whole nation had been made. But at the end, there were still about 99 out of every 100 Chinese on Taiwan that were bound for a Christless eternity.

What was still missing? Was it really even possible to make a disciple of a nation as the Lord had commanded us to do? I would go through one more highly successful/ deeply frustrating experience before I would find satisfactory answers to these questions.

Donald McGavran's Institute

Somewhat to my displeasure — especially when I learned I would have to raise all the funds — I was sent to study at the Institute of Church Growth during our first furlough in 1963. The Institute, which in two years would become the School of World Mission at Fuller Seminary, consisted of about ten students sitting around a large table in the library stacks of Northwest Christian College in Eugene, Oregon. Donald McGavran was the professor.

I suffered greatly during those months. The malaise, it turned out, was allergy to dust, paper and mold. It would have been hard to find a more suitable venue for the allergies to flourish than this setting amidst thousands of mostly old books.

But the course was life-changing.

The fledgling church growth movement provided all kinds of insights and tools for the discipling of nations.

One was the concept of responsiveness, the idea that there comes a time in the providence of God when a person, a family, a tribe, a people group and even sometimes almost a whole country becomes very open to the gospel. Having spent one year in the Philippines after our term in Taiwan, I wondered if that were not the case in that island country.

Under McGavran's close supervision, I compiled and graphed all the growth data available on about 75 denominations in the Philippines. Some were clustered around 50 percent increase in a decade, some around 100 percent. But three evangelical denominations were leaping ahead at a combined 536 percent growth in ten years.

This was hard evidence that the Church could grow very rapidly in the Philippines if it would only apply itself.

Returning to the Philippines in 1964, I began a study of one of those three denominations. I intentionally chose the one with the smallest missionary force and least financial backing. This turned out to be the International Church of the Foursquare Gospel. If I could find out why *this* denom-

26

ination with so few resources was growing, I reasoned, I would find how *all* denominations could grow rapidly and make a solid dent in the discipling of the Philippines.

The study eventually appeared in book form (*Fire in the Philippines*, now out of print). After interviewing more than 200 of the denomination's pastors and converts, I concluded that the growth was real, the converts solid. I also came in contact with the spiritual dynamic behind this rapid growth which I will return to in a later chapter.

But the specific method that seemed most directly related to this spectacular growth was the evangelistic home Bible study group. Filipinos with their large families in this Roman Catholic society enjoyed getting together in homes to examine the Bible. And when they did, many came into a personal relationship with Christ.

Here was one secret of growth that could be copied by tens of denominations and thousands of local churches. It was inexpensive, meeting places were readily available, laymen and women could be found in every church that could be "equipped" for this ministry.

If evangelistic Bible study groups was the method that would win the greatest number of people to Christ in the responsive Philippines, why not put thousands of Christians to work using it?

The Christ the Only Way Movement

My chance to do something about this idea came in 1968. As the newly appointed Field Director for O.C. in the Philippines, I was selected to join about 65 Filipino Church leaders in Singapore for the Asia/South Pacific Congress on Evangelism. The congress, by the way, was one of several regional meetings that flowed out of the Berlin Congress on World Evangelism in 1966.

When this Philippine delegation met separately in Singapore, it made a commitment to return home and do something about reaching its nation for Christ. As one representing an organization that specialized in mobilizing the whole body of Christ in whole countries, they turned to me for help.

Our partnership ultimately resulted in the All Philippines Congress on Evangelism in 1970. During this ten-day congress I was able to share the data that clearly demonstrated the tremendous responsiveness of the Filipino people as well as the evangelistic method that gave promise of reaping the greatest possible harvest.

I said to the 350 leaders in attendance that we ought to put "LEGS" to the Bible. That is, there was a great need to proliferate *Lay, Evangelistic Group Studies* of the Bible all over the country. Estimating there were probably 3,000 or so truly evangelical churches in the country (it was later determined there were a total of 5,000 protestant churches at that time), I suggested it should not be unreasonable to produce 10,000 LEGS within a few years. That would require only three or four such groups on average for every committed evangelical congregation.

Somewhat to my surprise, these leaders were challenged by this goal and committed themselves to it. They also set in motion a process by which the goal could be reached. A committee was formed with Nene Ramientos, one of my staff members in Philippine Crusades (O.C.'s name in the Philippines), as chairman.

Out of this came what would be called the Christ the Only Way Movement. The country was divided into 17 districts and a full-time coordinator appointed to each. Hearing of the project, Stan Mooneyham, then president of World Vision, committed himself to enlist missionary organizations to provide $100 a month for the salary of each of these men.

Through Mooneyham and others, the funds were raised and the coordinators selected one by one as district congresses on evangelism were held. After several training sessions, these coordinators began sharing the vision and teaching the LEGS concept throughout their districts.

As the months rolled by and reports filtered in, it was not at all evident that the goal would be reached. But through the coordinators, publications, evangelistic crusades (one for each district using associate evangelists of Billy Graham among others) and a number of related activities, ownership of the project and goal gradually came into being.

One creative idea stands out in my mind. My mission, Overseas Crusades, had pioneered the idea of sports evangelism, so it was a natural to think along that line. I wrote Bud Schaeffer, then head of the Sports Ambassadors department, about the idea of sending a basketball team for a full year. They could travel all over the country, train local churches in the LEGS approach, play games against the local all-stars and funnel the converts and contacts into local Bible study groups.

The team Schaeffer put together on arriving in the Philippines quickly dubbed themselves the COWboys (Christ the Only Way boys). In nine months they played before an estimated 200,000 people in about 200 communities and saw hundreds of LEGS started. In this and other creative ways the movement spread throughout the archipelago.

But would the goal of 10,000 be reached by the target date of March 31, 1973? We still seemed a long way off. When the date came and passed, reports from coordinators began to trickle in. With the arrival of the last one, the number of evangelistic Bible study groups totaled almost 11,000!

The goal had been reached. A major victory won. Tens of thousands of dollars had not been spent in vain.

Then why was I not elated?

Out of the desert?

It was the same old story, only worse. Now we had done the research, mobilized a major part of the whole body of Christ in a very responsive society around a method that seemed best suited and most productive in the situation, and had reached and exceeded the incredible goal of

10,000 evangelistic Bible study groups.

But out of 35 million Filipinos there were still very close to 35 million who did not know Christ personally.

Based on the experience and training of several years, we had developed a strategy that seemed to put together all the ingredients that should have led to the discipling of a nation according to the Lord's command, and the nation seemed hardly more discipled than when we began.

"Why, Lord," I began to pray over a period of weeks, "did you give us a command that you knew was impossible to obey? Did you deceive us? Did you mean something different than what your Word seems clearly to say?

"If you truly wanted the *nations* to be *discipled*, why didn't you stay here on the earth? You could have gone about every village as you did in Galilee. You could have gone speaking the language, wearing the dress, intimately knowing the culture, eating the food and having relatives and contacts in every village and neighborhood of every 'nation' in every country in the world.

"You could have gone demonstrating your power, showing your love and compassion and forcefully communicating your great message of the Kingdom. Why did you leave it up to us, when you knew it was totally beyond our capabilities?"

It was a daring prayer, but at least it was honest. For two thousand years the Great Commission had gone uncompleted, despite the incredible efforts and sacrifice of a select few in each generation. And yet, at the rate we were going, it did not seem likely we would be any more successful in the future.

At the height of what might have been considered my greatest triumph in ministry so far, I was immersed in gloom. Would I never emerge from the back side of the desert? Was there no light at the end of the tunnel?

The saying goes that it is darkest just before dawn. Would this be true in a figurative sense as well?

Chapter 4

The Best Method under Heaven

"Now that I have your attention," the Lord seemed to say after weeks of praying this prayer, "I want you to know that is exactly how to go about completing the Great Commission.

"See to it that I, the Lord, truly become incarnate, as you have been suggesting, in every small group of people on the earth."

In a flash of insight from the Lord it all became very clear. Where does the Lord now dwell?

"Christ in you, the hope of glory" (Col. 1:27).

"Greater is he that is in you than he that is in the world" (1 John 4:4).

"Where two or three are gathered in my name, there I am in the midst of them" (Mt. 18:20).

Christ could be alive and well and present in all his power and glory and compassion while communicating his wonderful message of the Kingdom in a totally contextualized way in every small community of people if only there were some truly born-again believers exercising the gifts of the Spirit and functioning there as the body of Christ.

The application to the Philippines was almost immediate. According to government statistics, there were about 35 million Filipinos scattered over the 7,107 islands of the archipelago. They spoke seven or eight major dialects and perhaps another 150 minor ones. There were 3.5 million Muslims, a half million Chinese and hundreds of thousands of tribals, among other smaller groups.

Furthermore, everybody lived in a barrio (Spanish term) or barangay (Tagalog term) whether in the city or a rural area. This was the smallest political unit in the country. Each had a barrio captain. These barrios were also quite homogeneous. Barrios usually consisted of people of the same language or dialect and frequently of the same basic vocation. Many rural barrios were made up of one large, extended family.

50,000 barrios, 50,000 churches

Since there were about 35,000 barrios for the 35 million people, their average size was around one thousand.

If Christ were to be incarnate within easy access both practically (in terms of distance and transportation) and culturally (in terms of language, vocation, economy, etc.) of every person in the country, there would have to be a gathering of the body of Christ in every barrio.

A church in every barrio! How many would that be? A total of 35,000.

But by the time 30,000 more were planted (there were an estimated 5,000 in existence), many years would go by, the population would grow and the number of barrios would increase, probably to about 50,000 by the year 2000.

The arithmetic was simple. The Church of the Philippines needed to plant 45,000 more churches by the end of the century to have one within easy access of every citizen at that time.

But wasn't this an outlandish thought? Not really. At least not in arithmetical terms. If the Church of the Philippines would plant new congregations at an Average Annual Growth Rate (AAGR) of just 10 percent, the number of churches would double every seven years. Since this was 1974, the number of churches could double almost four times by AD 2000. That would take them close to 60,000!

Ten percent AAGR meant only one church in ten would have to plant a daughter congregation in a given year. Or each church, including the new ones, would have to plant a new church only once every ten years. Given the responsiveness in the Philippines, the awesome task of planting 45,000 churches in 26 years almost seemed too easy when seen in this light.

Nonetheless, I was reluctant to share the idea with anyone. Would I not be laughed out of court?

On the one hand, the goal seemed outlandish, at least at first glance. On the other hand, was I not just stating the obvious? In fact, when I wrote a paper for the EFMA Executive Retreat in 1984 and alluded to this subject, one leader wrote me and said, "Isn't this what missions have always been doing, trying to multiply churches throughout a country?"

In reply I said something to the effect that while that was theoretically true, it was not what in fact was happening. The whole church growth movement came into being precisely because mission had turned to a hundred other good things that were taking it further and further from the primary emphasis of seeing men and women brought to Christ and the multiplication of new congregations. If Donald McGavran has said anything to the Church, it is this.

Birth of a movement

McGavran said this and a whole lot more when he came to the Philippines in 1974, the year I had fixed in my mind 50,000 churches by AD 2000. He was speaking at one of Dr. Vergil Gerber's Evangelism/Church Growth work-shops that Gerber was to hold in well over 50 countries.

If I remember correctly, the workshop was jointly sponsored by the Philippine Council of Evangelical Churches (PCEC), Church Growth Research in the Philip-pines (C-GRIP) and the Christ the Only Way Movement (COWM). But much of the leg work fell to Philippine Crusades under my leadership.

We brought together about 75 of the leaders most concerned for the growth of the Church in the Philippines. Each was required to bring 11 years of data for his or her denomination, and there was much sharing among the delegates. In particular, the Conservative Baptist and Southern Baptist growth programs that were already under way gave visible demonstration that growth of up to *20* percent a year was not impossible or even unreasonable.

Because of my heavy involvement in bringing the delegates together, I suppose, I was asked to give the final challenge at the three-day seminar.

It was now or never. After reviewing some of the teaching and information shared during the seminar, I suggested the idea of working most directly at the discipling of the whole nation by working towards the goal of 50,000 churches by the year 2000.

"I'm not in the habit of giving invitations," I said, "and I want you to think this over carefully. But if there are any here who would like to commit themselves and their organization to this goal, would you please stand."

To my utter amazement, everyone in the room instantly stood to his or her feet.

It was in that electrifying moment — though it was not so named at the time — that the DAWN movement that would eventually spread to every region of the world was born.

Another grass fire?

As church and mission history amply illustrates, however, enthusiastically setting a goal for completing the Great Commission, or at least a small part of it in our case, is a far cry from reaching it.

Would this be another *ningas cogan* (grass fire) as Filipinos so aptly named a very human trait? Would the idea burn hot and spread quickly only to die out just as fast?

Only time would tell — time, as it would turn out, when I would not even be in the Philippines. For our furlough was to begin in a few months, and, as the Lord seemed to say to me in another surprising moment of insight, I would never return to a resident ministry there.

In my new role as Director of Overseas Fields with Overseas Crusades, however, I did return with Bob Waymire, who would later become the founder of Global Mapping.

"By the way, Bob," I said to him as we flew into Manila from Taipei in 1978, "how about spending a few weeks in the Philippines to find out what has happened to the goal of 50,000 churches by AD 2000?" Four years had passed. Would we find any thing left of the dream?

The 1974 "elbow"

Bob Waymire stayed, and returned the next year as well. From his research came the book that I authored with Donald McGavran, *The Discipling of a Nation*. (This book is also now out of print.)

A line graph of his overall data clearly showed an "elbow" at the 1974 year.

For the 10 years prior to that year, a representative group of denominations had been adding members at a 5.6 percent AAGR and planting new congregations at a mere 1.7 percent AAGR. (The low church-planting figure in part reflected the loss of many churches in Mindanao because of guerrilla activity. Usually, as we will see, membership growth corresponds very closely with church-planting activity.) The respective AAGR's for the next four years were 9.7 percent and 10.1 percent.

The growth rate had doubled. The Church was growing at a rate that would take them to the 50,000 goal by the end of the century.

History was being made. Never before had a major portion of the body of Christ in a whole country banded together to reach a national goal that would call for a greatly increased rate of growth.

The book provided the resource material for a national congress on evangelism called for 1980. The 500 or more delegates who attended the two-part congress — about half meeting in Cebu City in the Visayan Islands and the other half in Baguio on Luzon Island — affirmed the national goal in a joint declaration.

Five years later a second congress was called. By now the movement was being officially sponsored by the Philippine Council of Evangelical Churches and was called DAWN 2000.

Data gathered by Philippine Crusades and presented at the second congress in 1985 clearly showed that the whole Church of the whole country was still growing at better than nine percent AAGR. After ten years, they were still just about on target.

Jun Vencer, chairman of PCEC, reported that by the end of 1984 there were 10,006 documented churches. Southern Baptist missionary James Slack in an independent research project estimated there were at least another 5,000 local churches that had not yet been documented.

In reporting his findings, Slack said, "If church growth is one strong indication of revival, then what is happening in the Philippines must be the longest revival ever."

DAWN 2000 after 14 years

In preparation for the third DAWN 2000 Congress held in October 1988, Tim Ellison of Overseas Crusades did perhaps the most extensive data collection to date. He found some discouraging trends, but also some very good news indeed.

The bad news was that the AAGR for 25 denominations about which he had gathered detailed information was down to 7.5 percent since the congress three years before. Since a rate close to ten percent was needed for the whole 26-year period, reaching the goal was in jeopardy.

But there were tons of good news as well.

For instance, there were five denominations growing at 15 percent or better per year, one at over 43 percent! Another seven were between 9.5 and 15 percent.

But the best news was yet to come. For Ellison also discovered — just as James Slack had — that there were literally thousands of evangelical churches in existence that were not connected with any of the denominations he had studied. The DAWN idea of multiplying churches had so permeated the thinking of Christian workers that it had become the natural thing to do.

So he added a conservatively estimated 5,573 to the 15,427 on his denominational lists, bringing the total to 21,000 at the end of 1987. This meant that 16,000 new churches had been added to the 5,000 in existence when DAWN 2000 began in 1974.

Furthermore, this amounts to an AAGR of 11.67 percent. If churches continue to multiply at this rate to the end of the century, the Philippine Church would actually consist of 88,185 local congregations, 38,000 above their target!

The enthusiasm evident at the congress tended to bear out the actual statistics. "I believe the greatest growth will come in the next ten years," said Jun Balayo, the O.C. national who has been working most closely with the movement since the beginning in 1974. Others expressed the same sentiment.

A follow-up meeting for about 150 top leaders was scheduled to make in-depth plans to see not only that there would be at least 50,000 churches in the country by AD 2000, but also that there would actually be at least one in every single barrio, including the currently unreached people groups in the country.

Is not this type of planning and church multiplication

exactly what is needed to complete the Great Commission in our time? A revival in part triggered by the Church of all nations committed to a goal of filling their land with congregations, with cells of believers?

Best method under heaven

Those who have studied in the church growth school of thought, of course, will remember the teaching that there are hundreds, even thousands, of good evangelistic methods. Principles remain constant but methods vary according to culture and a host of other circumstances.

Peter Wagner, now the leading proponent of church growth missiology, certainly sees the value of the many methods, plans and strategies for world evangelization. But he also makes it clear that one method supersedes them all. Wagner calls it the "best evangelistic method under heaven." He is referring, of course, to the multiplication of new churches.

In an article written a number of years ago, Ralph Winter of the U.S. Center for World Mission was responding to a student who asked about novel approaches to evangelism. He perceived she was really looking for tricks and gimmicks to attract attention. He replied that the extensive activity of starting new congregations was "the slickest trick of all."

"The care and feeding of new congregations is thus to me the central strategic activity to which all 'gimmicks' must be bent," he wrote.

In a more recent article, David Hesselgrave of Trinity Seminary expressed with some depth the same idea:

> Most Christians probably assume that to evangelize the world means to preach the gospel everywhere to everyone in every way possible. But when one carefully examines recent events and literature dealing with "evangelization" and related terms, such as "people groups,"

"hidden" peoples and "unreached" peoples, it is clear that the concept is not easily defined.

Out of all this discussion . . . somewhat of a consensus is emerging. People are "reached" (or evangelized) when, 1. they have had an *understandable* [emphasis his] hearing of the gospel, and, 2. when they are geographically and culturally accessible to a viable, evangelizing church.

Some experts stress only one aspect while others stress both. Personally, I think bringing together of the two ideas represents a "marriage made in heaven" because it is altogether too easy to settle for preaching the gospel and assuming that it has been understood.

Emphasizing establishment of a church assures us that at least some have understood the gospel and also makes possible continuing evangelization.[1]

Hesselgrave's words get at the heart of the DAWN strategy and the goal of 5 to 7 million more churches. To make sure that at least some have really comprehended the gospel in a given community, and to provide for the continuous evangelization of that community, requires that a church be planted in it.

Furthermore, as we moved on from the Philippines and began to see the DAWN strategy develop in other countries, we began to see that those denominations that grow most rapidly are usually the ones that put great emphasis on church multiplication.

We certainly found this to be the case in our studies of the Church of Guatemala.[2] One denomination, the Príncipe de Paz (Prince of Peace), provides a good illustration. It was the passion of its founder, José Muñoz, to multiply congregations. He constantly challenged his people to reach out to new barrios and neighborhoods. "The mission of the church is to plant other churches," he repeatedly said. He urged his pastors to plant one new church every year.

The result was that in just 27 years Príncipe de Paz grew from nothing to become one of the largest denominations in the country, overtaking denominations that had been there two and three times as long.

In our studies of all denominations in Guatemala we found a high correlation between church-planting efforts and total membership growth. When churches were being planted at a moderate rate, denominational growth was moderate. When church-planting rates soared, membership growth soared. When church planting was neglected, membership growth rates declined.

The Assemblies of God, for example, saw their membership grow by a moderate 145 percent (10 percent AAGR) from 1970 to 1980. This was accompanied by a commensurate 136 percent increase in churches. In 1981, however, growth of their total denomination increased by 23 percent in just that one year. They accomplished this by increasing their number of churches by a huge 34 percent!

The Church of God of Prophecy illustrated the point in a negative sense. They grew by an excellent 256 percent from 1970 to 1975. That this would not continue, however, was obvious since they increased their number of churches by a much lower 75 percent during that period. In fact, their increase in membership was only 65 percent in the next five years, which was accompanied by an even smaller increase in new churches.

The overall picture of the Church of Guatemala showed a remarkable correlation between membership growth and church planting from 1970 to 1980. During that period total membership of all denominations increased by 225 percent, and number of organized churches increased by an identical 225 percent.

This emphasis on the *method* of evangelism rather than on the number of converts seems to be a healthy approach. Many have said to us that it is presumptuous to set a goal for number of new converts, pointing out that only

God can convert a soul. We can present the gospel but the response to a considerable degree is out of our hands.

But when we emphasize church-planting evangelism, we are putting our emphasis on the method that will in the long run produce the greatest number of converts.

One of the outstanding growth programs in the Philippines — that of the Christian and Missionary Alliance — is an example of this. They developed one five-year project that focused on the goal of 400 new churches and a commensurate increase in new members. When they reached this goal for churches planted, they set a new goal for the next three-year period. This goal, however, was set in terms of new converts rather than new churches. When they fell quite short of their goal, they realized it was because they had shifted their emphasis away from the method that would most effectively bring in those new converts.

Some blind spots in the West

These illustrations, of course, come from the Third World. Westerners tend to have a much harder time seeing the need for more churches.

"There are churches on every corner already."

"We have enough struggling little churches."

"Surely the last thing we need is more churches."

These are the comments we have heard repeatedly while communicating the vision of DAWN in the U.S., Canada, New Zealand, Finland and other Western nations.

Such comments arise from blindness in various forms.

The need for evangelism

Sometimes there is blindness to the need for evangelism. There *are* a lot of struggling little churches out there. And if someone comes along with the excitement of a new church in the area, members can be siphoned off from existing congregations.

41

There is truth in this, especially since growth of many churches in the West comes as a result of transfer from one church to another. This is the marble effect — a lot of saints rolling around from one church to another, but adding little to the total number of evangelical members in an area.

But churches don't have to be planted through sheep stealing. There are vast numbers of people still outside of Christ and the Church in our Western countries.

We pointed this out to the churches of Santa Clara County in California. The existence of mega churches with attendance up in the thousands and smaller churches seemingly everywhere gave a false impression. Data gathered by Dan Griffiths and others of the RISE (Research In Strategic Evangelization) Committee in cooperation with CityTeam, a parachurch organization, in 1985 unveiled a completely different picture.[3]

It was found that on a given Sunday only 8.6 percent of the Anglo population of the Valley could be found in a protestant church of any kind. If the Lord could be concerned for the shepherd who had 99 percent of his sheep in the fold, how would he feel about the shepherds of Santa Clara Valley where 91.4 percent of the potential sheep were still outside the fold?

Furthermore, even if every pew in every church were filled, only 12 percent of the population could fit. Clearly, one problem was not having too many churches, but not having a concern for the lost and unchurched.

Look for "hidden" groups

A second form of blindness relates to ethnicity and other forms of homogeneity. If the situation was bleak among the Anglos in Santa Clara County, it was desperate for the 40 percent of the population that was non-Anglo. Only four percent of these residents were attending a protestant church.

For the county's 300,000 Hispanics, there were only 45

mostly tiny churches with a total of 3,475 members, barely 1.2 percent of their community. There were *no* churches for 930 Afghans, 8,506 American Indians, 6,000 Asian Indians, 566 East Europeans, 2,320 Ethiopians, 1,563 Guamanians, 1,608 Hawaiians, 4,000 Iranians and 617 Iraqis.

For additional tens of thousands who fell into such diverse categories as university students, street people, single parents, technocrats, prostitutes, foreign visitors of various kinds and many others, there was little or no hope for spiritual enlightenment.

The specifics will vary from county to county, state to state and country to country. But the underlying reality remains the the same. England, for example, has been called a post-Christian nation. Others have said that the working class in that nation was never reached in the first place. The truth is that the evangelical Church in Western lands has been blinded to the unreached condition of ethnic groups, economic classes, inner cities and homogeneous groups of all kinds that are still outside the boundaries of their ministries. Massive church planting is still the need of the day, even in the West.

Check the data

A third blindness relates to actual results. Again using Santa Clara County as an illustration, we found some good news buried in the raw data. It was that Anglo churches as a whole had doubled their AAGR from 2.3 percent in the 1976 to 1980 period to 5.2 percent in the next five years. Most of this growth, however, had taken place among nondenominational or independent churches. There were 15 of these in 1980 with 14,604 people in average attendance.

This attendance for nondenominational churches almost doubled in the next five years to a total of 26,231 for a rather astonishing AAGR (for the U.S.) of 12.5 percent. What was behind this remarkable, unprecedented growth? It was the planting of 16 new independent churches in this period of time. These new congregations accounted for 73.5

percent of total nondenominational growth in those five years. Furthermore, church planting declined in the next 18 months, and the growth rate for the total Church of the Valley fell to about the same 2.3 percent it had attained from 1976 to 1980.

Some of this growth came, I should mention, from non-denominational churches spinning off parts of their congregations to start some of these new churches (though at least one new church went from zero to well over 2,000 in this time). So if one were to add the growth of a daughter church to that of the mother, the total growth of that church would look very good.

In fact, this is an excellent way to keep track of and report one's growth. A mother church should not only be aware of its own growth record, but take pride in the total growth of its whole family of congregations — its daughters and granddaughters and on to succeeding generations. "Churches should get brownie points," says Peter Wagner, "for how many daughter churches they plant as well as for their own growth record."

But again, there was clear correlation between church planting and overall growth of the Church in an area.

Filled with the glory of the Lord

Studies from around the world could be mentioned that show this same pattern. Truly, the best method under heaven to get the maximum number of new converts into the Church is to put as many trained members as possible into the activity of starting new congregations.

New congregations provide the growing edge for a denomination. Each new church is a seed planted that yields 30-fold, 60-fold or 100-fold increase. Every time a new cluster of converts is gathered in an unchurched neighborhood or village, there is opportunity to reach out to friends, relatives and other close contacts. A new convert still has close ties with and considerable influence over these unbelievers. This is usually not the case in churches

44

with a long history in a community.

In the Old Testament we find a great prophetic hope expressed several times:

". . . all the earth shall be filled with the glory of the Lord" (Numbers 14:21).

". . . for the earth shall be full of the knowledge of the Lord as the waters cover the sea" (Isaiah 11:9).

"For the earth will be filled with the knowledge of the glory of the Lord. . ." (Habakkuk 2:14).

What is our part in filling the earth "with the glory of the Lord"? Are we not working towards this end when we set our sights on saturating every people and nation with local churches? Is this hope not fulfilled to a considerable degree when the risen, glorious Christ is made alive in every small community of people on the face of the earth in the form of a gathered cell of believers? Is this not the most direct way to work towards the completion of the Great Commission?

As I have tried to demonstrate, multiplying churches until a country is filled with them is not only good theory and theology for the discipling of a nation. It also is demonstrably the best and fastest way to grow and make disciples. All strategies for world evangelization and all methods of evangelism, in my estimation, need to so design their ministries that the planting of new churches is at least one primary outcome.

Focusing on a worldwide goal of 7 million new churches, then, can become a star to guide us. We will be truly working most directly and effectively at world evangelization, at giving every person on the face of the earth a real opportunity to decide for or against Jesus Christ, when all our many excellent strategies and methodologies center on this primary and crucial goal.

But why 7 million? Is it the right goal? Is it reachable? Am I really sticking my neck out too far this time? Maybe so. Let's take a look.

Notes

1. David Hesselgrave, "World Evangelization by the Year 2000?" *World Evangelization*, March-April 1988, p. 13.
2. Jim Montgomery, Emilio Antonio Núñez, Galo Vasquez, *La Hora de Dios Para Guatemala*, (Guatemala City: SEPAL, 1983). (English manuscript available from Dawn Ministries.)
3. Jim Montgomery, "Rise and Possess the Land," addresses given at the RISE Santa Clara County Congress, November 19, 1986. Manuscript available from Dawn Ministries.

Chapter 5

7 Million
Churches To Go

My original thoughts about the number of churches needed for the Philippines fell into some very simple arithmetical patterns. There were 35 million people in about 35,000 barrios. One church per barrio; one church per 1,000 people. Simple.

Bob Waymire and I shared this idea with David Barrett when we first met him in Nairobi in 1980. Barrett was then working on his monumental *World Christian Encyclopedia* which since has been published by Oxford Press. At the time, Barrett agreed that one church for every 1,000 people seemed about right as a goal not only for the Philippines but for the whole world.

I was interested to note, then, the first working drafts of a paper for the Global Consultation on World Evangelization by AD 2000 and Beyond held in Singapore during the first week of January 1989. It suggested a number of goals including one for church planting. It called for 3.5 million churches to be added to the current 2.5 million by the end of the century. This would bring the total to 6 million for a projected population of 6 billion: One for every 1,000 people in the world!

47

This was of particular interest not only because it was the same ratio I had decided on, but also because the same David Barrett was the primary resource person for the massive amount of data that was collected for this consultation.[1]

By this time, however, I had changed my mind and concluded that the number of new churches we should aim at planting by AD 2000 ought to be 7 million.

The idea gets more complicated

Further research and experience soon made it obvious that an average of one church for every 1,000 people could never be equated with the idea of one church in every village and city neighborhood for the world.

For example, during that same Africa trip where we first met Barrett, Ted Olsen, Bob Waymire and I took a trip back into the mountains of Cameroon. Along the way, we passed what must have been thousands of villages. On enquiry, we found they averaged 300 to 500 people. Each of these would need a church. And there must be multiplied thousands of villages in the world of about the size as these that ought to have their own congregations. One church per 1,000 people would not work for these villages.

Secondly, it soon became clear in the Philippines that many barrios actually had two, four or even six churches already and that new villages would be entered by more than one church-planting group. The 5,000 churches in the country in 1974 would therefore mean there were churches in perhaps much less than 5,000 barrios. So even if the goal of 50,000 churches were reached by AD 2000, this would still not mean there was one church in every barrio. Furthermore, since the population was predicted to reach about 80 million, we would not have one church for every 1,000 people either.

Then came discussions with Ralph Winter when he suggested that in reality in every village there are at least three distinct groupings of people that would require a separate church-planting effort. He mentioned India, for example, where there are actually several different caste groups in each village.

My conclusion was, then, that we might need many more village churches in the world than I had thought. On the other hand, it is possible that in the densely populated cities of the world one church for every 1,500 or so might suffice.

At any rate, to have at least one evangelical congregation in every village and city neighborhood for every class, kind and condition of people in the world would call for some other scheme than just saying one for every 1,000 people in all those groups.

Insight from the Ghana model

The same African trip that brought us to Cameroon and into contact with David Barrett in Nairobi also included another divine appointment that would have far-reaching consequences. This was with Ross Campbell, a New Zealand missionary with Worldwide Evangelisation Crusade headquartered in London.

Working under the leadership of the Ghana Evangelism Committee, Campbell had spent several years developing the New Life For All program into a powerful force in the Church and nation. With his growing staff of Ghanaians, materials and seminars had been developed and perfected to the point where tremendous growth was being experienced in participating churches. In fact, Campbell reported that a very high percentage of the churches that became involved doubled the size of their congregations within a year of the first seminar. Some grew by 1,000 percent in one year!

By 1980, they had a staff approaching 20 who were now working with an incredible 2,000 churches. There were some problems that came with this growth, however. The more churches that were added to the program, the more there was need for additional staff. That placed increasing pressures on fund raising and administration. And there were still many thousands of churches in Ghana that desperately needed their help.

What was the answer?

After sharing the DAWN idea with Campbell, he quickly concluded this represented the next logical step for their national strategy. Instead of just trying to go physically to every church in the country with their *training* programs, they would also move into the arena of trying to *motivate* the whole body of Christ to get moving on their own.

When, after our departure, he presented DAWN to the Ghana Evangelism Committee, they also embraced it. In line with DAWN thinking, they concluded, according to subsequent materials, that the Great Commission could be most directly fulfilled in their land when there was: 1) "an active, witnessing cell of believers in every village, town, urban neighborhood and ethnic community in the country;" 2) "a church for every geographical group of 300 to 1,000 people;" and 3) "a viable church within geographical and socio-cultural reach of everyone."

With great energy and creativity, Campbell gave himself and his staff to this new direction. They divided the country into eight regions and proceeded to treat each region as a separate "nation." Each region would develop its own DAWN-type project by carrying out research, putting the data together into a large folder and holding a "DAWR" (Discipling A Whole Region) congress.

At this regional congress, delegates would gather by denomination towards the end of the week to set their regional goals and plans for church multiplication. When all eight regions had completed this process, there would be a consultation for the whole country.

To find out just how many churches would be needed, a massive research effort was made in each region. Tens of thousands of dollars were raised within the country. This was spent primarily on the salaries of their four full-time and 11 part-time staff put into this aspect of the work.

Armed with a Church Growth Survey Questionnaire, a Locality Survey Form and an Unreached/unchurched Villages and Towns Form, young men fanned out to visit every town and village of 50 or more people. The amount of firsthand information gathered was vast.

They gathered basic information about the number of churches, average attendance and growth rates for each local church and for each denomination. This is standard information for a DAWN project and forms the basis for the first DAWN Congress in a country.

But they also gathered information that ultimately is needed for every land. In 49 pages of data for just the first region they listed the following:

1. every locality with its subdivisions
2. the population of the locality and its subdivisions
3. the number of each kind of church (nonindigenous non-Pentecostal, nonindigenous Pentecostal, Seventh Day Adventist, Roman Catholic and African independent)
4. the percent of each major ethnolinguistic group.

Armed with this data, leading pastors and denominational heads could see how many churches were needed of what kind and exactly where to plant them. At the first regional congress, held in the Brong Ahafo region, many groups, therefore, set numerical goals and in some cases actually listed the names of villages and towns where churches would be planted in the coming year.

With data gathered for all eight regions, a national congress was held in the spring of 1989. At this congress they were able to present a precise enumeration of communities *without* a protestant church:

223 towns with a population over 1,000

496 villages of 600-1,000 population

1,917 villages of 300-600 population

12,075 villages of 50-300 population.

This total of 14,711 was rounded off to 15,000 unchurched communities. To this they added another 4,000 to
make their faith projection a total of 19,000 new churches
by the end of 1996. This would give them a total of about
38,000 churches by that date, or an average of one for each
443 people in their projected population of 16,800,000.

When this is accomplished by 1996, there will truly be
"an active, witnessing cell of believers (evangelical
church) in every village, town, urban neighborhood and
ethnic community in the country," as some of their literature describes their goal.

This would include saturation church planting among
all the 100 or so language groups of the country, some of
which have been very lightly reached with the gospel and
others of which have been virtually unreached — including
various Muslim groups.

To the DAWN way of thinking, they will then have
reached the penultimate measurable goal for the discipling
of a whole nation and all its people groups. *Everyone* will
be within easy access of a cell of believers who are incarnating — although imperfectly — the Lord Jesus Christ.
Everyone will have an optimum opportunity to accept or
reject our risen Savior.

Projecting the whole world

This very detailed research approach is not necessary
to *begin* a DAWN project. In a later chapter we will discuss
the relatively small amount of data that needs to be
gathered to successfully launch DAWN. As we will see,
the amount can be relatively small *if it is the right kind of
data.*

At the same time, the kind of research that has been
accomplished in Ghana needs to be done ultimately in
every country. Precise information about every unreached
people and every unchurched community gives an exact
battle plan for the discipling of all nations.

But we don't have to wait for all that information to be

gathered to make a projection by faith concerning the number of churches that need to be planted in the world by AD 2000 in order to have one within easy access of every person of every class and kind and condition of people in the world.

I have been suggesting the number 7 million more. Added to the current 2.5 to 3 million in existence, this would give us a total of up to 10 million by the end of the century, or on average (a somewhat ambiguous idea as we have seen) one for every 600 people.

Reaching a total of 10 million churches of the right kind and scattered in the right places by AD 2000 may not give us the precise number needed to fully church the communities of the world. But mobilizing the resources of the Church around such a goal could very well ensure our working *most directly* or at *optimum endeavor* toward completing the Great Commission as speedily as possible.

The next question that must be answered, however, is whether such a goal is within our grasp. For that we turn to the next chapter.

Notes

1. This data appeared in the book *Seven Hundred Plans to Evangelize the World* by Barrett and James W. Reapsome. It was published by New Hope, the Southern Baptist Press in Birmingham, Alabama.

Chapter 6

Is It a Reachable Goal?

The eight-hour meeting at the Hyatt Regency at the Los Angeles Airport held May 18, 1988, overflowed with promise. About 15 of us had been brought together by Thomas Wang, Executive Director of the Lausanne Committee, to talk about world evangelization and the year AD 2000. Each of us was involved in plans that had targeted that date for reaching some very major goal towards the completion of the Great Commission. Out of this initial meeting came the Global Consultation on World Evangelization by AD 2000 and Beyond held in Singapore, January 5-8, 1989.

But as the conversation flowed back and forth, one of our leading missiologists attending made the statement that immediately caught my attention. "If people are given a worthwhile goal they believe is within their reach," he was saying, "they will give their lives for it."

To plant 5 to 7 million more churches in the remaining

years of this century would require just that — men and
women who would give their lives for it. Multitudes of
them. Committed believers who would live for the multiplication of churches, and, perhaps, many who would die
for it.

Assuming for the moment the worthiness of a goal that
would attempt to "fill the earth with the knowledge of the
glory of the Lord" by planting a church incarnating Christ
among every group of 600 or so people in the world by AD
2000, we must ask the next question: Is it achievable? Is it
within our reach?

Nothing, of course, is too hard for God. And I do believe
that as the DAWN strategy catches on in every country of
the world, such a goal will definitely be within our reach.
But before we go on to examine just how DAWN can
contribute to planting 7 million more churches, let's take a
look at some of the existing realities that might suggest
whether a such a goal is reasonable or not.

Just three new churches each

In the first place, let's assume there is one evangelical
congregation for each 53 active, adult believers in the
world, a figure Bob Waymire calculates as being fairly
close to reality. By church growth rule of thumb, there are
about 2.5 times as many believers in the Christian *community* of a church than there are members on the roll,
giving us an average Christian community of 132 per
church.

Diving this by the estimated 330 million believers in
the evangelical community in the world at the end of 1987,
we calculate about 2.5 million churches. This is the same
number used by David Barrett and others. We have no
exact count of what would be considered evangelical
churches by our definition, but this figure is probably not
far from wrong. In that case, to plant 7 million more
churches would require each existing congregation to plant
three more by the year 2000, hardly an impossible task.

It will naturally be argued that existing churches would be inclined to plant new churches nearby and among their own kind of people. If that were the case, even if all existing churches did their part by planting three more, there would still be millions of communities in the unreached and lightly reached peoples of the world without a cell of believers.

We would therefore have 7 million more churches, but not necessarily in the right places.

So let's modify the challenge and ask every existing church to plant not just any three, but one E1 church, one E2 church and one E3 church. Let me explain.

One church would be planted in a nearby unchurched community that is culturally of the same kind of people. This community might be of a different social or economic level, but still of the same general culture. This would be E1 evangelism carried out by members of the congregation.

A second outreach would be planting a church in a somewhat different culture. It could be in a nearby ethnic enclave, a cultural group some distance from the church or even in a different country. Depending on the circumstances, this E2 church would be planted by church members or by missionaries sent out by the church.

A third outreach would be more vicarious. Each local church could be so encouraged to participate in the prayer and financial support of missionaries going to a completely different culture that at least one outcome would be the planting of at least one new church by AD 2000. Few local congregations could fully support such a missionary. But by their support of denominational or independent missionaries and mission societies, they could participate vicariously in the planting of at least one E3 church in the next 12 years (from the end of 1988 to the end of AD 2000).

When we further discuss the DAWN strategy, we will see just how it can be expected that millions of churches around the world could be motivated and trained to plant three more churches each in the next dozen years. For now, we're just looking at the simple arithmetic. Assuming local churches around the world could be so motivated and trained, the task of planting 5 to 7 million more congregations in the places where they are needed certainly is not out of the question.

Increase from 8 to 11 percent growth

Let's take another mathematical viewpoint. To add 7 million more churches to the estimated 2.5 million for a total of 9.5 million by AD 2000 requires an Average Annual Growth Rate (AAGR) of just under 11 percent. In some small and responsive nations like Guatemala, this is already happening. In China, the world's largest, it is already being exceeded!

In the West — where there is open opportunity for evangelism and church planting — the figure for the most part is much lower and other countries will fall somewhere in between.

But what is the current AAGR for the whole body of Christ worldwide?

No one had this information, so I asked Bob Waymire to calculate it. He and his colleagues at Global Mapping had developed a chart of the estimated growth rates for the Church of every country in the world by comparing data produced by David Barrett, editor of the *World Christian Encyclopedia*,[1] Patrick Johnstone, author of *Operation World*[2] and several other scholars who had current data from various nations. After publishing this data in the July 11, 1986, issue of *Christianity Today*, Waymire says no one challenged his conclusions for any country except for the growth of Pentecostals in the U.S. A recent study, however, proved Waymire's data was accurate on that point as well.

It had not previously occurred to Waymire, however, to total this information for the Church of the whole world. Going back over the data, his staff at Global Mapping was amazed to discover that the estimated rate of growth for the whole evangelical Church worldwide was about 8 percent! I would have guessed maybe half that. I wonder if any missiologists had any idea it was that high. This is good news of the highest magnitude.

Assuming churches multiply at about the same rate as the overall membership growth of churches — a proposition we will look into further in another chapter — we can say, then, that evangelical congregations of every sort are already multiplying at an AAGR just three points lower than the required 11 percent needed to reach the goal of 7 million more. To put it another way, we would have to multiply congregations 37.5 percent faster than we currently are.

Furthermore, even without any increase in AAGR for new churches, we could expect about 4.3 million more to be planted worldwide by the end of the century just at the current rate of growth. That would account for 61 percent of the goal right there!

This calculation is based on there being 2.5 million churches at the end of 1987. As we saw in the last chapter, there could actually be a lot more churches than that. And when we get to defining what we mean by a church in the next chapter, the task will perhaps seem even easier. Furthermore, if our goal in reality were placed at somewhere between 5 and 7 million more churches, our needed AAGR would be even less.

It is not impossible to imagine, however, an aroused, revived Church worldwide increasing its church-planting rate to 11 percent a year. If planting seven million new congregations in 12 years required an AAGR of 20 or 30 percent, say, we might conclude from a mathematical standpoint that was impossible. But 11 percent is not.

Crusade's one million

If mathematics is on our side, so is what is actually happening right now in the real world. In fact, many groups are already taking on sizeable chunks of that goal.

Campus Crusade for Christ is one of them. Speaking to the National Religious Broadcasters Convention in February 1988, Bill Bright announced plans for a cooperative effort to help "take the gospel message to every person by the year 2000."

The strategy, called New Life 2000, emphasizes working with Christian churches and ministries throughout the world. "No single group could possibly fulfill the Great Commission alone," said Bright. "We desire to serve as a catalyst to help unite Christians in the task of world evangelism and the fulfillment of the Great Commission in this generation."

Campus Crusade is not only trying to help mobilize the Church of the world in this task but is focusing each of its 40 sub-ministries on this strategy as well. Some of their objectives include:

- 271 major language and 1,000 dialect translations of the *Jesus* film;

- 5,000 *Jesus* film teams by 1995;

- 5,000 New Life Centers to train 200 million new Christians to share their faith;

- 10 million New Life Groups for home Bible study and spiritual nurture;

- a "prayer target" of helping one billion people receive Christ as Lord and Savior.

Given their track record, who would bet against Crusade accomplishing these goals?

What is really new and terribly exciting, however, is one final goal of the New Life 2000 strategy. It is this: "assist denominations with their growth goals, *resulting in the establishment of more than one million new churches!*"

Campus Crusade has now caught the vision of church multiplication as a necessary step in world evangelization and has committed its very considerable resources and expertise to it. And in typical Crusade style, it has set a quite significant goal.

In fact, their goal alone represents 14 percent of the 7

million churches being suggested.

With about 22,000 denominations in the world, according to David Barrett,[3] there certainly is a huge repository for Campus Crusade to choose from in finding denominations to assist with their growth goals.

The Southern Baptist share

Even without any special efforts or training programs, however, many denominations are already out of the starting blocks. The Southern Baptists with the largest missionary force of any denomination in the world, for example, have launched their Bold Mission Thrust program. Their overall objective is to reach "every living person in the world with the gospel by the year 2000."

They also have reemphasized the multiplication of churches as a primary step in this program of world evangelization. The goal agreed upon in 1977 was a ten-fold increase in churches from 1976 to AD 2000. That would mean growing from 7,500 churches to 75,000! Part of their strategy is to see that 70 percent of their 3,800 missionaries in 113 countries devote at least one half of their time to church planting.

Two Pentecostal projects

Though the Southern Baptists have the largest denominational missionary force, the more rapidly growing Pentecostal denominations are also catching the AD 2000 fever.

J. Philip Hogan, Division of Foreign Missions Executive Director for the Assemblies of God, for example, recently wrote that he is "witnessing a growing awareness among church leaders that the end of the age is upon us. It's time to believe that the Church of Jesus Christ can complete its mission on earth."

The Assemblies are certainly doing their part. At the

end of 1987 they reported 15,816,435 members and adherents meeting in 115,623 congregations in 120 countries outside the U.S. These are very conservative estimates, as by their own admission some of their national Churches do not count women as members, many do not count young people under 18 and some do not count people at all! In publishing their data, however, they list only what is actually reported.

Their data going back to 1975 shows their national churches have been growing at an AAGR of 11 percent for this 13-year period to the end of 1987. At this rate alone they will add slightly more than a third of a million — 334,387 — new churches by AD 2000. It is also this rate, you will remember, that the worldwide body of Christ must grow at to reach the 7 million new churches by the end of the century.

So as I've said, the Assemblies of God are already doing their part. But don't figure on them continuing *only* at this rate. For they have set in motion a new evangelization and church-planting program for the end of this century called Decade of Harvest. For this program, their U.S. Church has already set a goal to plant 5,000 more churches, and their 120 national Churches are in the process of setting their goals. Hogan says it might take up to a year before they have reports from all their fields concerning their goals, but it would be quite surprising if they were not considerably above the 11 percent they have been averaging for at least 13 years.

"We intend to reach the 2.7 billion people who have not heard about our Lord, and we pledge to do it by AD 2000," says their brochure. "We dare to believe that God has established this Fellowship all over the world for the greatest evangelism the world has ever seen."

Fire like that tends to spread. As more and more leaders start "daring to believe," the goal of 7 million more churches is going to seem more and more reachable.

In 1982, leaders of another Pentecostal denomination, the International Church of the Foursquare Gospel, set a number of major goals to be reached by 1990. This program, called Harvest Vision 1990, really got them going. Six years later, according to Phil Starr, their Communications Coordinator, they had increased the number of countries they were working in from 37 to 62, their worldwide membership from 740,000 to 1.4 million and their number of churches and meeting places from 7,817 to 19,000!

By 1986 they were planting one new church every six hours somewhere in the world. In 1987 they planted one new church every *two* hours!

Things were going so well that in 1988, when they held an international conference for leaders from all 62 countries, they developed a whole new set of goals for the year 2000.

Among other things, they targeted 99 new countries, 3 million new members and *62,000 new churches and meeting places!* To meet this goal they would have to grow at an average annual rate of about 12 percent, slightly above the needed rate for all denominations.

Nor is the Foursquare Church content to work only where the gospel has already gone. For among their goals set in 1982 was that of launching work among at least 100 hidden people groups with hopes for up to 160. By 1987, however, they had already entered *176* hidden peoples that produced 5,394 converts and 416 churches. Their vision for the unreached is now stretched way beyond these goals.

Other denominations, both Pentecostal and non-Pentecostal, have developed strong evangelism and church-planting programs for their fields around the world. And surely the idea will spread. With 22,000 total protestant denominations in the world, it is not unlikely that we will see a host of programs proliferate that have church multiplication as at least one primary activity.

As will be discussed in a subsequent chapter, such denominational programs represent perhaps the most effective vehicle for a vast multiplication of churches in the world. As hundreds and thousands of denominations catch a vision for goal setting and church growth projects, they will provide the key to the planting of 7 million more churches.

China's one million

Even this possibility, however, does not exhaust the potential for the Church worldwide reaching 7 million more congregations. The land of China gives us great hope in several ways.

The Lord had so prepared a harvest and so equipped his Church that probably the greatest ingathering in the history of Christianity has taken place in our time. This happened after all the missionaries were kicked out, after the Church suffered immense persecution and after we in the West presumed it was all but dead.

Yet, when the veil was lifted, it was seen that tens of thousands had been turning to Christ. Ralph Winter says that "careful estimates exceed 50 million believers." Most China experts agree this is a conservative number. The actual number could be much higher, and of course the Church continues to grow each year. In fact, Winter calculates that in recent years the Church there has been growing at an AAGR of 14 percent![4]

Furthermore, if we divide the conservative 50 million believers by the worldwide average of 132 per congregation, we would find close to 380,000 churches in China.

Some experts say this is high. A frequently quoted figure has been 50,000 house churches. But that figure would put about 1,000 people in each house church. Those must be some houses! If there are 50,000 houses owned by Christians that can each accommodate 1,000 people, maybe the communists did a better job than we thought!

Of course, there are churches other than house churches and these are jam-packed with many hundreds every service. But that still doesn't account for all those believers.

I talked with Jonathan Chao of the Chinese Church Research Center in Hong Kong about this. The Scandinavia Publishing House in Copenhagen will soon release his book *The Church in Contemporary China* where he gives a fascinating picture of what is actually happening. Chao told of personally visiting house churches with 100 to 300 attending. On average, rural churches would be somewhat smaller.

If we assume an average of 200 in attendance country-wide, there would be about 250,000 congregations of all sorts and sizes. Chao himself says his center estimates a ten-fold increase in number of churches from 1949 to the present, putting the current figure, he said to me, "between 200,000 and 300,000."

Now if 250,000 churches were to proliferate at the same 14 percent AAGR as church attendance has in recent years, the total number of churches in China would increase by about 1.1 million between 1987 and AD 2000!

In my conversation with Chao, I found him very conservative and reluctant to speculate on the future. "We simply don't know what will happen," he said. "Circumstances might come that would slow the growth of the Church." Presumably, other circumstances could speed the growth.

At any rate, the overall growth of the Church from 1949 to 1987, when there were many years — perhaps even decades — when growth was very slow if not negative, has been 11 percent. Even assuming there would continue to be good times and bad, could we not expect at least an average 11 percent annual growth rate?

If that were the case, there would still be about 720,000 new churches added for a total of about 970,000 or close to a million by the end of the century. This would provide China with almost one church for every 1,000 citizens.

And it must be remembered that this remarkable growth has taken place spontaneously under the sovereign hand of God in one of the most difficult situations in the world for the Church to flourish! Cannot we expect God to continue to grow his Church in China? Cannot we expect God to do more of the same in other difficult spots?

A breakthrough in Japan?

Speaking of difficult spots, let us turn to the nation of

Japan. After decades of excellent work by a host of missionaries, the Church is still less than one half of one percent of the population of 122 million. Average church attendance for the 7,000 congregations is calculated at less than 20!

And yet there is a growing air of expectancy in that ancient culture. Besides some evidences of responsiveness and some growth here and there, there is the vision of Paul Yonggi Cho. He is the pastor of the Korean church that grew from the original four people attending in 1958 to become the largest single congregation in the world. Peter Wagner, who has just returned from visiting that church as I write this, reports membership now at 600,000 supported by an estimated 50,000 house churches that meet during the week.

Cho is now poised to fulfill a vision the Lord gave him in 1978 of seeing 10 million Japanese coming to Christ by the year 2000. Given his background of achievement, who is going to stand up and say this goal is beyond him? Cho has already become fluent in Japanese and has sent some workers to Japan. One church has already exceeded 2,000 in attendance after just three years. Sixty percent of this congregation is composed of Korean expatriots, but 40 percent — close to 1,000 people — are converted Japanese. This is the equivalent of 50 Japanese churches of the current average attendance!

This congregation quite naturally is built on the same pattern as the mother church in Korea; that is, it has a proliferation of house churches. If Cho does reach his goal of 10 million by AD 2000, and if we assume the same international average of 132 in the Christian community per church, we would see over 75,000 new congregations spring up! If you take average attendance as the same 15 to 20 that the house churches in Korea exhibit, the total number would be considerably higher.

Admittedly, there are a lot of ways to play with these numbers, but here again we have evidence of the Lord speaking to one of his choice servants about a vast increase in the harvest with an implied vast multiplication of churches.

India: one million more

Another difficult spot is the land of India. However huge and difficult the task may seem, there is now a working committee of capable and respected leaders who have envisioned the goal of one church in each village and city neighborhood of India by AD 2000. This amounts to about 600,000 villages and 400,000 neighborhoods or a total of one million churches.

Bobby Gupta, who is following in his father's footsteps as the president of Hindustan Bible College in Madras, is one of the leaders of this movement that is based on the DAWN model. In his own ministry at the college he has developed a strong missionary training department with a goal of 1,000 churches planted in ten years.

But he also identifies at this point another 170 organizations that have either the potential or an actual program in operation that could plant 1,000 churches each. "All we need is to raise up a total of 1,000 such organizations that will each plant 1,000 churches and we will reach our goal of one million," says Gupta.

Most of this church planting will of necessity be cross-caste and therefore cross-cultural. Fortunately, India already has a strong tradition of mission societies that have been sending missionaries by the hundreds to multiply churches across the subcontinent.

"We might not reach the full one million," Gupta said to me recently. "But I see a great revival sweeping our land much like that of China. Certainly there will be many hundreds of thousands of churches planted before the turn of the century."

The challenge of the Muslim world

Of course, the most difficult situation of all is the

Muslim world. Our relative neglect of these Islamic peoples is a scandal. Had we put commensurate resources into their evangelization, we might now be poised for a mighty harvest among them.

But things are changing. I like one of the slogans formerly used by the Frontiers mission under the leadership of Greg Livingstone: "Muslims. It's their turn." Maybe we are finally going to make the effort necessary to bring these nations to Christ.

Don McCurry is another one among a growing number who are committed to the discipling of the Muslim world. He is the founder of Samuel Zwemer Institute, named after the pioneer to the Muslims in the last century.

At the Edinburgh conference of mission heads from around the world in 1980, McCurry committed himself to see that a church-planting movement be started in every Muslim people group by the year 2000. Not only has his commitment remained firm, but he has now extended his vision to a "more thorough goal of saturation church planting" in every group. He is currently working closely with Dawn Ministries and has formed a sister organization — Ministries to Muslims — with this sole commitment in mind.

God is raising up the McCurrys of the world for just such a push as this.

Nor are we devoid of emerging models to reach Muslims.

The "One, One, One" project in Indonesia is an example. Under the visionary leadership of Chris Marantika, who is partially supported by Partners International, this program sets its sights on planting "one" church in each "one" village in "one" generation. This would amount to 50,000 or 60,000 churches by AD 2015 in the largest Muslim nation in the world with a population of 175 million. We'll come back to this project and its likelihood of success in another chapter.

Admittedly, Indonesia is a majority Muslim nation in the non-Arab world and therefore easier to reach. On the other hand, there are more non-Arab Muslims than Arab in the world today.

Furthermore, who knows how close we are to a major breakthrough among Muslims? There is certainly a lot of trauma in that part of the world, the kind of trauma that has brought on great responsiveness to the gospel in other settings. The recent discrediting of the Shiite Muslims in Iran through their loss in the eight-year war with Iraq could send ripples of discontent and therefore greater responsiveness to many Islamic nations.

Realistically, it might take an additional ten or 20 years beyond the end of the century to saturate Muslim nations with cells of believers. But if we don't include them in the goal, we surely will not make the prayer and resource commitment necessary to reach them.

Church planting through radio

There is another major plan in the works that attacks the problem from another sector of the battlefield. It relates to the technologically advanced world of the media.

In the fall of 1985, an agreement was signed by the three largest missionary radio ministries in the world (HCJB, FEBC and TWR). It read, in part: "We are committed to provide every man, woman and child on earth the opportunity to turn on their radio and hear the gospel of Jesus Christ in a language they understand, so they can become followers of Christ *and responsible members of his Church by the year 2000.*"

The emphasis on the last phrase, of course, was added by me because it is quite significant. It signals an end to the philosophy of radio ministry that says, "We will just broadcast the message and leave what happens to the Lord." Now they have publicly gone on record as implying they will so design their programming that people will actually become followers of Christ and, furthermore, that these converts will become responsible members of his

Church.

Now it is hardly possible that a convert can become a "responsible" member of the Church of Jesus Christ without belonging to a local congregation. This further implies a lot of people coming to church and, in the final analysis, a lot of new churches being planted.

But there is more than just an implication. For representatives of the same organizations have helped form RICE and placed John Gray of FEBC as director. "RICE" is an acronym for "Radio In Church-planting Evangelism." It is the specific intention of this organization to do the research and make the recommendations leading to programming that will actually result in churches being planted.

Now there is at least the potential for missionary radio not only to bless and equip the existing believers, to increase responsiveness to the gospel by gaining the favorable attention of great numbers in a population and to invite people to make a decision for Christ in their homes. Now there is the possibility that radio can and will train new believers in how to get together with other believers and form themselves into little house churches, many of which will become more than just that.

This has already been happening, of course. David Barrett says there are 39,750 radio churches in Russia alone, another 16,300 in India and a world total of 76,625.[5] Dick Hillis, who spent 17 years in China and later founded Overseas Crusades, credits radio with much of the vast multiplication of house churches that has already taken place in China. "It was Acts chapter eight all over again," says Hillis. "Persecution scattered the believers throughout the land. Where they ended up, they began meeting in little Bible classes. But the nurture and development of these little groups into 300,000 house churches was done almost entirely by radio."

And it is in such situations that radio can perhaps be most useful in producing thousands of new churches. That is, radio might turn out to be very successful in multiplying churches in situations of limited or no access from church planters outside the group. We can imagine this would be one way church multiplication movements could be started in the Muslim world, for example.

The unreached peoples movement

Another major force for completing the Great Commission in our time dates back to the Congress on World Evangelization held in Lausanne, Switzerland, in 1974. It was in Lausanne that Ralph Winter presented his landmark paper on the unreached peoples of the world.

In the meantime, Winter has established on a former Nazarene campus — now worth more than $25 million — the U.S. Center for World Mission in Pasadena, California. This growing institution is wholly dedicated to seeing a church-planting movement established in every one of Winter's estimate of 16,000 unreached people groups in the world by AD 2000. The "Mission 2000" plan of the Center states that "there are ample evangelical resources in the world community to make a serious attempt to plant the church within every people by the year 2000."

Though the slogan is to "Plant the Church within every people group by the year 2000," the idea extends beyond that. "You can only make a slogan so long," says Winter. "What we have in mind really is the starting of a *church-planting movement* in every people group and the continuing of the movement until the people groups are filled with congregations."

As the mission forces of the world — including the emerging wave of Third World mission societies — are increasingly mobilized for this task, we will see additional tens and hundreds of thousands of churches planted — and "in the right places," too.

As chairman of the board for the Center, it has been my profound joy to see not only the miraculous provision for the purchase of the campus but, more importantly, the vision of entering all the unreached peoples become almost a household concept among evangelicals the world over. Now that the campus is paid for, there is an astounding network of volunteers who can and will be mobilized for the task of world evangelization.

Many other plans

I have a growing list of groups, some large, some small, around the world that have set challenging goals for church planting. In the process of writing this chapter, a number of growth projects have come to my attention.

For example, Peter Wagner has just returned from a trip "down under" where he spoke at the New Zealand DAWN Congress and in some pastors' seminars in Australia. While in Australia he attended the Christian Outreach Center of Clark Taylor where he heard the following story:

In 1974 Taylor started to build a church from scratch. By 1988, that church had grown to a membership of 4,400 meeting in a sanctuary that seats 5,000. Actually, he had planned to put up a building that would seat 40,000 which would have been the largest auditorium of any kind in the South Pacific! But the Lord made it clear to him he should build a seminary instead. It would be better to train pastors for new churches than to simply increase the size of his congregation.

The result was that in that same span of 14 years, 135 new churches were planted by his students. With this background, he now has determined before the Lord to plant 100 more churches in 1989 alone. Thirty of these will be in other Asian countries.

Looking farther down the road, Taylor envisions church-planting projects in 85 countries as well as starting one church for every 8,000 Australians by the time he reaches age 75 in 25 years. By my calculations, this would be about 2,500 more churches.

As Wagner reported, "Taylor is almost a one-man DAWN project all by himself!" If individuals such as Taylor can envision the planting of 2,500 or 10,000 more churches, we can expect this to be multiplied by 30-fold, 60-fold or 100-fold (10,000 percent) when the whole body of Christ of whole nations is mobilized for a saturation church-planting project.

With stories like this popping up on a regular basis from points all over the world, it appears all the more that a vast multiplication of congregations is much on the mind of the Lord.

Perhaps there are also tens of thousands of local pastors and laypeople upon whom the Lord has given the burden to plant one or two or ten or 100 new churches.

Whether all the great and small visions of all God's people add up to 7 million more churches by AD 2000 or not, we do not know. It seems to be a spontaneous movement inspired in part by the church growth school of thought that has permeated the thinking of churchpeople all over the world in recent years and in part by the approaching end of this century. The latter certainly gives us a significant milestone for worldwide mobilization of the body of Christ. Surely the movement is also coming from the heart of God.

Perhaps Phil Hogan's observation that there is "a growing awareness among Church leaders that the end of the age is upon us" has more substance than dream. And as we approach the end of the age, can we not expect the Church of Jesus Christ to be mobilized and equipped for one last big push?

It can be done!

There are other trends and movements that give further encouragement to those committed to completing the Great Commission in our time. Certainly the explosive growth of missions among Third World churches is one. With the exuberance of the young and assuming they are committed to church multiplication when they go out, we can expect further reinforcement in working towards a goal of 7 million new churches.

The deepening interest in prayer as well as what Peter Wagner calls the third wave of the Holy Spirit are other forces being mobilized for this task.[6] In the final chapter I will write further about the undergirding spiritual dynamic that must be present in the Church.

To wrap up this chapter, I'll admit to a certain amount of conjecture and perhaps unwarranted optimism — something I am occasionally accused of. The potential of some of the areas and projects perhaps has been overestimated. Others possibly were underestimated.

The intent was not, however, to give precise mathematical proof that reaching 7 million more churches by the end of the century is in the bag. Rather, it was to show that such a goal is not unreasonable.

While there is not at this point a consensus of leaders around the world on this particular goal, it does seem that the Lord is laying pieces of it on the hearts of many: One million here and another million there. Seventy-five thousand here, 100,000 there, a third of a million with another group and tens of thousands in this situation and that. Major national and international projects here and there that imply further multiplication of churches.

With the resources we now have, with the plans and programs being dreamed and put into operation and with the anticipation of a mighty move of the Spirit in our time, it should be clear that a goal of 7 million more churches — one within easy access of every person of every class and kind and condition of people on the earth — is reachable.

We *can* fill the earth with the glory of the Lord by strategically placing cells of believers incarnating Christ in every village and neighborhood among every people group in every country if we *will*. And we can do it by the end of the century.

With this bold assertion, I conclude this chapter. It is my hope that the reader can see that even with present activities and trends, enhanced by the Spirit of the Lord, the idea of planting 7 million more congregations by the end of the century is at least not unreasonable.

So let us now turn to a discussion of the principles behind a mobilization movement that has already demonstrated its ability to increase the rate of growth of the Church of a nation. There is still much work to be done in filling the gap between what is now happening — 8 percent average annual growth — and what needs to happen — 11 percent average annual growth — to reach the goal of 7 million more churches by AD 2000.

Notes

1. David Barrett, ed., *World Christian Encyclopedia,* (Oxford, New York: Oxford University Press, 1982).
2. Patrick Johnstone, *Operation World,* (Gerrards Cross: WEC Publications, 1986).
3. Barrett, op. cit.
4. Ralph Winter, *Mission Frontiers,* January 1988.
5. Barrett, op. cit., data compiled from pages 133-771.
6. Peter Wagner, *The Third Wave of the Holy Spirit,* (Ann Arbor: Servant Publications, Vine Books, 1988).

Chapter 7

Some Basic Definitions

So far in Part One of this book we have been trying to describe just what DAWN *is*. It is a strategy for world evangelization that attempts to mobilize the whole body of Christ in whole countries around a goal for the number of churches that need to be planted by a certain date in that country. When this is accomplished, we have suggested that the Church is now working as directly as possible toward the discipling of its nation and all the people groups within it.

When the Church of *every* country has an intentional plan for saturating its land with cells of believers — one for every 400 to 600 in rural villages and one for every 1,000 to 1,500 in its cities distributed among all the cultural, ethno-linguistic and societal groupings of the land — we will be in high gear for completing the Great Commission in our time.

While the goal for every country will have to be decided by the Church of that country, a world goal of 7 million more churches planted in the right places seems to me to be about right. On the one hand, it is a goal both challenging and reachable and on the other, it is about the total needed to place an evangelical congregation within easy access of every person in the world by AD 2000.

There is already much going on that suggests such a goal is within our reach. At the same time, the point of this book is that such a goal should not be left to chance. We need a comprehensive, systematic plan in each country of the world so that the Church can be mobilized and put to work toward such a goal.

DAWN, we have suggested, is such a plan.

When we get to this point in our seminars on DAWN, however, we find people have many questions about the terminology and definitions we use in the DAWN strategy. Before going on to Part Two and a discussion of the principles behind DAWN that make it work, then, we will pause to clarify some of concepts we have been using.

"CHURCH"

An understanding of how DAWN defines "church" is fundamental to any challenge to plant 5 to 7 million more churches. If by "church" is meant a solidly built edifice with plenty of parking space, a full-time, seminary trained pastoral staff and a fully-orbed program of ministries for every age group and every interest, the goal will be a bit out of range.

I'm impressed with how a group of Christians faced this most fundamental question in China:

> Concerning [this] question, many older Christians said that they could not predict the future form of Chinese churches. So they turned to the Bible for an answer. They found in the Bible that the house-church form was a legitimate church.

> Paul mentions a house church in I Cor. 16:19: "Aquila and Priscilla greet you warmly in the Lord, and so does the church in their house" (NIV); also in Col. 4:15 "give my greetings to the brothers at Laodicea, and to Nympha and the church at her house."

> Later, we found a book by Wang Ming-dao
> [perhaps the most highly respected believer in
> China who languished in jail for more than 20
> years] on the institution of the church. He held
> that where there were Christians, there was a
> church. We were happy about this. We assumed
> that, although our group consisted of only a few
> people, we actually were a church, and our head
> was Jesus.[1]

"Where there are Christians, there is a church," is a
profound definition, coming as it does from a Church growing rapidly and laboring under the most difficult of circumstances.

The DAWN idea is to see Jesus Christ become incarnate
in every small group of mankind. How many believers does
it take to incarnate our risen Lord? Jesus said that ". . .
where two or three are gathered in my name, there am I in
the midst of them" (Mt. 18:20).

The goal set in 1966 and reported by Ed Dayton that I
mentioned previously suggests we ought to work toward
"ten witnessing Christians in every town of more than 500
people."

Two or three committed believers could possibly impact
50 or 100 others. Ten witnessing Christians in time could
perhaps reach out effectively to 500.

To call such groups of two or three or of ten a "church"
might be stretching it a bit. In our thinking, by minimum
definition there is a church when at least a small group of
believers led by an elder meets on a regular basis for
worship, instruction, the basic New Testament sacraments
and for witness and service. Where they meet, whether or
not they pay their pastor and like questions are not of
particular concern for our definition.

Denominations, however, tend to have a few more
requirements. Most would include a minimum number of
active adult believers that might range anywhere from
five — as is the case of the rapidly growing Southern

Baptists in Southern India — to 50. Some distinguish between "chapels" or "meeting places" and "churches" with the type of meeting place being a determining factor. Some draw the line based on whether or not the pastor is ordained and others have various combinations of these.

DAWN does not try to bring uniformity or impose any definition on the Church of a country. However, so as not to end up comparing oranges with apples, we suggest for statistical purposes the inclusion of all congregations of whatever definition. This would *not* include evangelistic Bible study groups or home groups that meet for fellowship as an additional activity to church attendance.

But it is some such definition of "church" as this that we have in mind when we suggest 7 million more are needed in the world.

A higher number?

With such an understanding of "church," by the way, it is quite possible there are many more churches in the world than generally thought. By personally visiting 142 of the 328 municipalities of Guatemala, for example, Overseas Crusades missionary Roy Wingerd and his young team found 1,800 churches that were listed nowhere on anyone's record. Since these covered mainly rural areas and only 43 percent of the country, his researcher's hunch is that there are an additional 2,500 churches in the land that statisticians are unaware of.

This total of 4,300 undocumented congregations would add 50 percent more churches to the total of 8,500 that are already listed. This is the same ratio that James Slack of the Southern Baptists found in the Philippines. Through his research a few years ago, he found about 10,000 churches on denominational rolls, but estimated there were another 5,000 that were on no one's list, again adding 50 percent to the total. In an in-depth study of two regions of the Philippines in 1988, Tim Ellison of Overseas Crusades also found 50 percent more churches in existence than were accounted for on any denominational records.

It could well be, then, that the total number of churches in the world is already much higher than thought, making the number of new churches needed less than 7 million. We could even revise the goal to say "7 million more *newly documented and/or newly planted* churches." This would make the goal even more within our reach.

Do we need more little churches?

Some ask, however, if we really need a lot more struggling little churches in the world. Others question whether the multiplication of tiny churches like this can truly lead to world evangelization.

For one thing, as Donald McGavran says, the only way to get a lot of grown men is to have a lot of little boy babies. Most churches don't emerge fully grown.

But, more importantly, even a congregation of 20 adult believers filled with the Spirit and on fire for evangelism can impact a village of six or seven hundred people over a period of time. If that's the kind of church it is, it won't remain tiny and struggling for long.

Are they mature churches?

This frequently brings up another question: How does the DAWN strategy make sure the newly planted churches are nurtured and trained so they become fully Christian in every sense of the word?

For this, the DAWN strategy relies completely on the denominations and missions involved. It is up to them to so develop their programs and train their church planters that strong churches emerge. We believe that truly evangelical denominations that have a desire to see people converted, brought into their churches and nurtured to maturity in Christ will find a way.

DAWN follows the General Patton approach: "I never tell my generals *how* to do something," he wrote in his

81

autobiography. "I tell them *what* to do and they come up with all kinds of ingenious ways of getting it done." We put this in the spiritual framework, of truth about how to plant churches that will grow strong and firm.

"PASTOR"

One of the first questions raised in the Philippines was where all the pastors would come from for these 45,000 new churches. There were about 70 Bible schools and seminaries at the time, most graduating three or four or up to a dozen or so each year. Where would so many new schools, dormitories, classrooms, professors and administrators come from? How could enough students be found and their tuitions paid? The dollar cost alone for all these would be way beyond the resources of missions and churches in the Philippines.

Where *will* 7 million more pastors come from? The answer, in part, depends again on our definition of "pastor."

In this also we look for minimum biblical requirements. These tend more in the direction of spiritual gift, spiritual qualifications and appointment by apostles than to academic achievement.

As in the definition of "church," DAWN does not attempt to impose any definition of "pastor," leaving this likewise to the denominations involved. Denominations that have a will to multiply churches always find a way to provide enough pastors, however they define the term.

A model from Bohol

Rudy Trigo of the March of Faith in the Visayan Islands of the Philippines is an example. My account of his training program in *The Discipling of a Nation* gives evidence to that:

In 1970, Trigo left the Pentecostal denomination through which he had come to know the Lord and been trained for the ministry. The denomination was doing well, but he believed it could grow much more rapidly. To develop his ideas, he felt he had to begin his own group.

He started with one church that year. Eight years later he had 220 churches with around 13,000 members. Another 7,000 people were meeting in close to 1,000 evangelistic home Bible study groups.

Where did he get all those pastors in so short a time? In 1973 he started a Bible school with 23 students. Tuitions for many were paid in sacks of rice or in $10-a-month contributions that came as a result of his trip to the U.S. that year. Students began by clearing the hillside donated by a relative of Trigo's and then by helping construct classrooms and dormitories made partly out of native materials.

When I visited this rustic campus in 1974, it was still without electricity. One Coleman kerosene lamp provided their only light source. Students went to bed at night and dressed in the morning in the dark.

Students found such conditions not much different from their rural homes, however, and they seemed to thrive under Trigo's rigorous program. Fired with his enthusiasm — and the joy of their conversions — they arose before dawn for Bible study and chapel, attended classes and worked the school's vegetable and animal farm during the day and studied and attended another chapel service in the evening.

Weekends brought no respite. They lasted three days and were spent witnessing, singing, evangelizing, leading worship and starting evangelistic Bible study groups. Some students walked or traveled by bus or jeepney, but some took to the growing fleet of 15-horsepower pump-boats to begin reaching the 70 islands surrounding their island of Bohol.

Rather than discouraging potential students, the almost frantic pace seems to attract them. The student body reached a peak in 1975 when 110 young people jammed the makeshift facility beyond reason. "I tell young people we don't have room, but they come anyway," Trigo told me in 1974.

Overcrowding was partially solved when Trigo sent one whole class into full-time ministry for a school year before it returned to complete its course.

Some will surmise that the three-year aca-demic program under these circumstances would not turn out fully qualified pastors. Perhaps not. At least not "fully qualified" to run sophisticated middle-class city churches. But they are highly qualified in basic training in the Word, in min-istering to the real needs of rural folks, in making disciples through evangelism and training in discipleship and in multiplying rural churches.[2]

In the interview, Trigo also indicated he gave his pastors further training through a daily radio program that covered the island. Here is a reminder that perhaps training pastors through this medium might prove an answer for countries and peoples otherwise inaccessible.

With respect to radio, China again comes to mind. Brent Fulton writes in *Mission Frontiers*[3] about Jonathan Chao and his staff at the Chinese Church Research Center in Hong Kong. "Chao began studying the condition of the Church in China in 1978 and concluded that the greatest need among Chinese believers was for leadership training," he writes. "To help meet this need, he launched the

'Seminary of the Air' broadcasts, which provide daily theological training on a level that rural lay leaders can understand."

Fulton goes on to list a number of broadcasting organizations that are not only developing similar programming but providing cassette tapes and literature as well.

But going back to the model from the rural Philippines, we see it is based on several principles that can be applied to any situation:

1. It draws potential pastors from the ranks of the newly converted. It must be assumed that in every group of new believers there are some who have the spiritual gift of pastor/teacher, even as Paul found elders from among his converts. The denomination that is evangelizing, then, has a pool from which to draw its new elders and pastors for the new churches.

2. The combination of apprenticeship and formal training is ideal. Graduates of his seminary know how to be pastors because they have been exercising various pastoral gifts all during their student years.

Growing denominations around the world usually have some form of this approach. Some are effective in training laypeople for evangelistic Bible study groups. When they have a proven ministry, they are ready for leading a little house church. With this frequently comes periodic short-term seminary training or theological education by extension. There are many models that are based on this combination of formal training and hands-on ministry.

3. Prospective pastors were not taken out of their economic and cultural settings, so there was no problem in their going back to the barrio. Pastors are needed for middle and upper class people and for city churches as well, but the principle remains: Don't isolate pastoral candidates from the world they have come from and will return to minister in.

4. Trigo was creative. He took what was available, whether free land or a local radio station, and developed a training program that produced the pastors he needed in

85

his situation.

5. Trigo communicated a great zeal for evangelism and church planting. When people catch this vision, there will be pastors enough.

We have tried not to give a precise definition of "pastor" but rather to suggest that a biblical definition of the term will not stand in the way of planting 7 million more churches. Finding enough pastors is not an insurmountable problem as rapidly growing denominations around the world continue to prove.

"EVANGELICAL"

Here is another bothersome term. With my background as a Conservative Baptist, my inclination is to say we need 7 million more "evangelical" churches. But who is an evangelical, and how can we count evangelical churches throughout the world? Some would remind me there are "evangelicals" in the Church of England, in the Lutheran Church and among Roman Catholics and Seventh Day Adventists to name a few. At the other extreme, some would throw out Pentecostals from the ranks of evangelicals!

In a DAWN project we want to see the *whole* body of Christ mobilized in a country. But we take "body of Christ" quite seriously. We want to see every born-again believer evangelizing the unsaved. We are not interested in seeing churches multiplied other than those filled with Bible-believing converts wholly surrendered to Christ.

Bob Waymire has introduced other terminology that I believe is helpful. He speaks of the "harvest force" and the "harvest field." The harvest force consists of all those who truly belong to Christ, who are "saved," regardless of their organizational affiliation. The harvest field, by contrast, refers to the "unsaved," all those who are not born again and not on their way to heaven.

For ease of understanding and communication, we refer to evangelical churches in this book, then, as those congregations predominantly made up of the saved, the born again, the "harvest force." By the way we define "church" and "pastor," it is easy to see that "evangelical" churches can and will be found in places other than traditional evangelical denominations.

It can be seen, then, that for statistical purposes it will be hard to arrive at a precise number of "evangelical" churches in some situations. But careful research among obviously evangelical denominations will yield fairly precise information to which can be added conservative estimates of other evangelical congregations.

How ecumenical is DAWN?

Some, however, will be interested not only in how we count evangelical churches but also in who will be included in a cooperative DAWN project.

Our concern is to mobilize the whole "harvest force" to reap the whole "harvest field." So a DAWN project will be developed by leaders of this harvest force. At the same time, DAWN cannot be carried out in a corner. If people are motivated through the efforts of a DAWN project to plant churches other than truly Christian, we cannot stop them.

In Guatemala, Amanecer (Dawn) has stirred up the Roman Catholic Church to a strong "re-evangelization" program. In Malawi, it is reported that the Muslims have started what amounts to a DAWN project of their own. "I saw with my own eyes," reports Johan Combrinck of South Africa, "how they have mobilized their resources to build a mosque within easy walking distance of every person in the country."

In the Philippines we saw a denomination on the fringes of evangelicalism greatly accelerate its growth rate after DAWN 2000 was well under way. Some would throw this group out of the evangelical camp entirely.

We cannot control who is going to be motivated by DAWN to do their own thing. Yet there are some safeguards.

In the first place, each national committee composed of leading evangelicals makes the decision as to who is invited to a DAWN congress. They know best who does and does not truly belong to the household of faith in their country.

In the second place, the message of DAWN is quite clear: it is a determined effort of church planting through extensive evangelization. The groups that might be objectionable to evangelicals in most cases disqualify themselves. It is hard enough to get *believers* to evangelize, let alone nominal Christians!

What about Pentecostal cooperation?

Another question related to the evangelical matter is this: Isn't it difficult to get Pentecostals and non-Pentecostals to work together in a project for church multiplication?

Yes. The walls between these two camps are usually — but not always — quite high. In one Asian country, a DAWN project is being developed that almost completely excludes Pentecostals. Despite every effort, no way has yet been found to bring them together. But it might turn out to be the only DAWN project where a schism to this extent exists. In another Asian nation, there is almost no distinction between Pentecostal and non-Pentecostal!

In the Third World in particular, there is usually another strong "camp" as well. This consists of the mainline denominations that are still much more conservative than their counterparts in the West.

Actually, we proceed on the premise that every true believer somewhere down in his or her heart wants to work with the whole body of Christ. Otherwise, I question if this person *is* a believer. Can one truly be born of the Spirit and hate the rest of the body that Christ himself has formed?

Finally, we overcome most of the divisions between the camps by focusing the unity around the national goal rather than around an effort to force groups from a wide variety of backgrounds into a common project where they have to rub shoulders on a regular basis. This approach really works as we shall see in a later chapter.

"NATION"

In a recent article in *Mission Frontiers* Magazine, I made the statement that "I sometimes wish the word *DAWC* were as beautiful and filled with such warm and pleasant connotations as the word *dawn*. DAWC is the acronym we would get if we were talking about discipling a whole *country*. But who would come to a *DAWC* congress or commit himself to a *DAWC* project?"[4]

So we've called it *DAWN*, Discipling A Whole *Nation*, even though we're really talking about whole countries and all the people groups or "nations" within them. We are well aware that the "nations" Jesus refers to in his final command are not the same as the geopolitical entities we call "countries" today.

We see in the book of Revelation, for example, that it speaks six times of the people "from every tribe and tongue and people and nation" (5:9, 7:9, etc.). The children of Israel, of course, consisted of 12 tribes or "nations." In Joshua 23 we see that all the kings or cities in the land of Canaan are repeatedly referred to as "nations."

Applying this terminology to the world today, we find most countries are composed of tens or even hundreds and in some cases thousands of such "nations." Missiologists refer to these as "people groups," "peoples," "ethnolinguistic groups" and sometimes "homogeneous units," among other terms.

Throughout this book it should be quite clear when we are referring to whole countries with the term "nation" and when we mean a people group within a country.

"UNREACHED"

Related to the term "nation" or "people group" is the

idea of *unreached* people groups. People frequently ask what the difference is between the DAWN concept and the unreached peoples movement.

The dream of starting a church-planting movement in every unreached people group of the world by AD 2000 is a missionary dream in the classical sense of the term. It comes from Paul's goal of preaching the gospel where it had never been preached before. Missions in this sense is pioneer work. In recent decades when so much of the "missionary" force has been directed towards helping the existing Church, the original idea has lost much of its force. The passion of Ralph Winter, among a growing number of others, is to rekindle this classic definition and arouse the Church of the world to complete the missionary task of starting a church-planting movement in every unreached people group of the world.

The task of saturation church planting in a country or in the world cannot be completed without the pioneer work of planting the first congregation in hundreds and thousands of unreached groups.

I was so challenged by this concept, first presented on a world level at Lausanne in 1974, that I became one of the early members of the Board of Directors of the U.S. Center for World Mission and continue to serve as its chairman.

But DAWN goes on to the task of what McGavran refers to as "evangelizing out to the fringes." The Great Commission is not couched in terms of only good beginnings in all nations but the *discipling* of all nations. DAWN keeps in mind the whole task of the Great Commission by challenging the Church of a nation to plant a church not only in every people group but in every village and neighborhood of every people group.

The DAWN strategy is designed to see that every people group and homogeneous unit is "reached" in every country. For when the Church is working at saturating the whole country with congregations for every 400 to 1,500 people in every class, kind and condition of its citizens, the reaching of people groups is being included in the task.

Another way to look at "unreached" from the DAWN viewpoint is to think of unchurched villages and neighborhoods. Each unchurched village is "unreached" by the incarnate Christ if there is no group of practicing Christians in it.

"VILLAGE AND NEIGHBORHOOD"

As with other definitions, we have trouble being very precise in saying exactly what is meant by a church in every "village" and "neighborhood." What comprises a village? How big is a neighborhood? As we have seen, villages can be thought of as having as few as 50 people. "Neighborhood" can be thought of as every floor of every high-rise in some cities.

The question becomes particularly pertinent when we are asked: How do you keep more than one group from planting churches in the same village?

It can't be done, of course. Since Dawn Ministries is not in charge of any project, we can only suggest. DAWN encourages every denomination and local church to do its own research. Each entity ought to be looking for a village, a neighborhood, a somewhat different homogeneous group where a church — or churches — needs planting. We also challenge the John Knox organization (see below and chapter 14) to do the kind of research that will uncover unchurched groups throughout a whole country.

In the end, however, each church or denomination will make its own choices. And what if more than one church is planted in a village or neighborhood? That's not all bad. An Assemblies of God church might reach some that the Southern Baptists will not. In India, as was mentioned earlier, there usually will be several different caste groups all in the same village. Several churches in one village might be the answer, or one church of one caste group in a village that reaches out to those of the same caste in nearby villages.

But I hope the reader by now is so convinced of the need

for at least one church in every small group of 400 to 1,000 to 1,500 people that you and your organization will act accordingly.

"DAWN VIS-À-VIS E.I.D."

One missions professor asked: "Isn't DAWN just another Evangelism in Depth (E.I.D.) or saturation evangelism program such as New Life For All in Africa? Is there a qualitative difference from these predecessors?"

DAWN grew out of the Christ the Only Way Movement in the Philippines which clearly was an adaptation of E.I.D. as practiced in Latin America. An even more direct antecedent was the Evangelism/Church Growth workshops held by Vergil Gerber in more than 50 countries in the '70s.

DAWN stands squarely on the shoulders of these great movements, but there are several emphases that were not seen in most implementations of E.I.D.:

- DAWN is built on thorough contextual and institutional research;
- It is a long-range strategy of up to 25 years or more rather than a one- or two-year program;
- It emphasizes completing the task of the Great Commission in a country rather than just proclamation or growth;
- It includes the more recent understanding of people groups and the discipling of the still unreached groups in a given country;
- It mobilizes the whole body of Christ around a nationwide goal rather than a number of set activities;
- It focuses on saturation church planting rather than saturation evangelism;
- It puts denominations and local churches to work in their own backyards rather than pulling resources out of the Church into unified projects;
- It encourages parachurch organizations to work truly alongside churches in developing their evangelism and church-planting ministries.

DAWN was not created out of thin air, but grew out of the methodologies and circumstances of our time. It does seem to be, as more and more leaders are saying, "the next logical step for the discipling of our nation."

"JOHN KNOXER"

As far as the DAWN strategy is concerned, the person we call a "John Knoxer" is the key to world evangelization.

The idea, of course, comes from the great reformer whose heart's cry was "Give me Scotland or I die." Dawn Ministries has picked up on this cry and is looking for that individual who similarly prays, "Give me my country or I die."

It must be more than a prayer, of course. Such a person must also have the spiritual gifts, the experience, the respect of national Church leaders and, most importantly, the organizational structure for mobilizing the Church of a nation in a DAWN project.

Such John Knoxers have now been located in more than two dozen countries in the last four years. The goal of Dawn Ministries is to have identified a John Knoxer for every country of the world by 1995 so that there is a DAWN project under way in every country at least by AD 2000.

After teaching the concept of DAWN and the John Knoxer to an adult class in Morgan Hill, California, for four Sundays, one layman said, "What this class has done for me is greatly reduce the size of the task. I can't comprehend reaching five billion people, but breaking the task down as you have makes it seem quite do-able."

Finding and equipping the John Knoxer of every country who can rally the whole body of Christ in that country for a DAWN project breaks down the task of discipling all nations into a manageable proposition. Country by country, the Church can be mobilized to the task of seeing that every person of every grouping can be within easy access of an evangelical congregation and thus be in the optimum position of deciding for or against Jesus Christ.

There will be more about the selection, training and functioning of John Knoxers in chapter 14.

"CLOSED COUNTRIES"

Will DAWN work in such "closed" places as the Muslim and communist worlds?

A few months ago, Don McCurry called and asked this same question. McCurry is one of the leading specialists in Muslim evangelism in evangelical circles. He spent many years in Pakistan, founded the Samuel Zwemer Institute and more recently Ministries to Muslims, developed the "Reaching Our Muslim Neighbors" seminar that is the best in the world on the subject and has done extensive research and travel in Muslim countries.

Being aware of all this, I was reluctant to give my answer. *I should have been asking him!*

"Theoretically we believe it will work anywhere," I answered with some hesitation. "We believe the principles are basic and scriptural. It is just a matter of modifying the procedure to fit the situation."

"I thoroughly agree," he said, much to my relief.

In fact, he agreed so strongly that we have in effect sublet the responsibility of developing a DAWN project for every one of the 44 majority Muslim nations in the world to McCurry and his new organization, Ministries to Muslims.

"I believe national leaders for these projects can be found," he says. "Wherever I travel in Muslim lands, I find Muslim converts who have the commitment and ability to develop DAWN projects. They also know what it will cost them."

As if in corroboration of McCurry's comment, I recently received a letter from one of the top church leaders in Pakistan.

"I want to offer my humble services for advancing this [DAWN] project in Pakistan," he wrote. "Doors are still open for us to communicate the good news to all who have not yet accepted the Lord Jesus Christ as their personal saviour.

"I don't know how long these doors will remain open. Why not make the best use of these opportunities? The wind of the Lord is moving and there is encouraging response. The [DAWN] vision will be accomplished in this part of the Muslim world. I will be ready to assist you to make this project meaningful for the people of Pakistan."

Not too long after the call from McCurry, I sat down with Peter Deyneka and his wife, Anita. Deyneka is president of Slavic Gospel Mission which was founded by his father. So Peter is to the communist world what McCurry is to the Muslim world.

The Deynekas were friends of ours from Wheaton College days, but they knew almost nothing about the DAWN strategy. After about 45 minutes of dialogue about it, Peter and Anita agreed that Poland would be the first country in Eastern Europe where DAWN should be undertaken.

"We can invite leaders from Russia who can take it back to their country as well," said Peter. They went on to discuss how DAWN could spread throughout the communist world. I hadn't yet asked whether DAWN was possible in their part of the world when they began planning how it would be accomplished!

In theory, I had believed DAWN, with necessary modifications, would work anywhere. Now these experts were telling me I was right and committing themselves to help make it happen.

I haven't yet heard from experts on such places as China and Albania, but I won't be surprised when I do. Maybe the answer for them will be radio or leaders working from outside the country.

Or maybe it will be just a continuing act of the sovereign will of God such as the "DAWN" project now going on in China, headed by the best possible leader. For the vast multiplication of churches taking place there under the direction of the Holy Spirit is exactly what we want to see in every country of the world.

By the above definition of terms and answers to some basic questions, it should be clearer that the idea of planting 7 million more churches by AD 2000 is not as preposterous as might seem at first glance. The chapter should also have reinforced an earlier comment that the number "7 million" is a rough estimate. Further research and refining of terms might suggest a more precise number. But, in my opinion, that is not necessary. The goal is close enough for the purpose of mobilizing the body of Christ in country after country to a massive new thrust of church planting as we work toward making available the incarnate Christ in the midst of every small grouping of people in the world.

Notes

1. Jonathan Chao, *Wise As Serpents, Harmless as Doves: Christians in China Tell Their Story*, edited by Richard Van Houten, condensed excerpts printed in *Mission Frontiers*, June 1988.
2. Jim Montgomery and Donald McGavran, *The Discipling of a Nation*, (published by *Global Church Growth Magazine*, 1980), pp. 99-103.
3. Brent Fulton, "China's Three-self Church: Tool of God, Tool of the Party," *Mission Frontiers*, June 1988, p. 6.
4. Jim Montgomery, "The Challenge of a Whole Country," *Mission Frontiers*, August 1987, p. 4.

Part Two

Why DAWN Works

Chapter 8

A Comprehensive and Systematic Plan

How then can we mobilize the whole body of Christ in the whole world in order to plant not only 7 million churches but 7 million in the right places so that there is one within easy access of *every* person in *every* situation in the world? So that every unreached people group has been entered and every nation is being discipled through the multiplication of churches?

That is where the DAWN strategy comes in. It divides the world into manageable segments, does the necessary research, mobilizes the whole body of Christ around an appropriate goal for its segment and distributes the work to effective structures already in existence.

In Part Two of this book, then, we turn to a discussion of the principles on which the DAWN — Discipling A Whole Nation — strategy is built. We feel DAWN puts together in synergistic relationship 12 powerful ingredients that combine to make it a mighty force for the planting of 7 million more churches and ultimately for the completion of the Great Commission.

A word of caution

This strategy, as we have seen, was developed literally over a period of decades. It has grown and matured on the spiritual battlefields of several countries. It is not the product of an ivory tower experience.

Through the decades it has been refined so that it can be expressed quite simply. As a result, leaders frequently "catch" it and commit their lives to it almost in an instant of time.

Such was the case of Johan Combrinck of South Africa. He had been studying in the States for five years, had been offered several very challenging and comfortable ministries but had accepted none of them. After about a five-minute explanation of the DAWN concept by fellow South African Johan Engelbrecht, however, he realized he had found his life's calling. He dropped the doctoral thesis he had been developing, changed it to a research project for DAWN in South Africa and joined the organization Engelbrecht had developed for the discipling of their homeland.

Its very simplicity and attractiveness, however, could lead to premature implementation of DAWN projects. The leader who feels a prompting of the Lord to develop a DAWN project needs to make a profound and long-term commitment. What is being presented is an overall strategy for mobilizing the Church of a whole nation in an in-depth, multi-year program.

Beginning such a program without adequate understanding or preparation could lead to truncated results, to denominations and countries being inoculated *against* any further attempts to disciple the nation, to a discrediting of the movement and the loss of its great potential for bringing multitudes into the Kingdom.

So if you are a reader of this book whom the Lord is leading to proceed with a DAWN project, we will rejoice! But we urge you to do so with great care. Read the rest of this book thoughtfully and prayerfully. Our experience leads us to believe that each aspect of the DAWN process is so interlinked with every other part that to eliminate or slight any one could ruin the whole. You will have to adapt the program to your particular situation, but I urge you to make changes in the approach only after the Lord has laid a deep conviction on your heart to do so.

FIRST FIVE POWERFUL INGREDIENTS OF DAWN

In this chapter, we present the first five of the 12 powerful ingredients that make up the DAWN strategy. We will simply mention the first two, as they have been thoroughly discussed in chapters one through seven:

1. DAWN IS CHRIST CENTERED.

In seeking to bring about the incarnation of Christ among every small group of people in the world, we are putting him at the heart and core of the strategy. The second ingredient flows out of the first.

2. DAWN FOCUSES ON THE "BEST METHOD UNDER HEAVEN."

Saturation church planting, we have tried to show, is the most direct way to bring in the greatest number of new disciples. In the DAWN way of thinking, all methods should lead to the multiplication of churches.

In this chapter we want to take a more careful look at

three more of these foundational concepts of DAWN that seem to make it so effective. These are ingredients three, four and five.

3. DAWN IS ROOTED IN THE *COMPREHENSIVE* PURPOSE AND PLAN OF GOD.

The Word of God consistently reveals the comprehensive purpose and plan of the Lord to see all nations and peoples turn to him. This great yearning of the Lord is expressed over and over in every section of both the Old and New Testaments.

Comprehensiveness in the Old Testament

The first such reference in the Pentateuch goes all the way back to Genesis 12:3 where the stage is set for all subsequent history. Almost at the very beginning of the Bible the Lord promises that through Abraham *all* the nations of the earth shall be blessed. To add to the significance of this promise, it is repeated four more times in the book of Genesis (18:18; 22:17-18; 26:4; 28:14) and mentioned in the New Testament as well.

In the history section of the Old Testament we find Solomon's very long prayer on the occasion of the ark of the covenant being placed in the newly completed temple. In the midst of this prayer he asks that all foreigners be blessed when they visit from a far country and then states the purpose for this blessing: ". . . in order that *all* the peoples [or nations] of the earth may know thy name and fear thee, as do thy people Israel" (1 Kings 8:43).

In the poetic books we frequently come across passages that deal with God's concern for and ultimate victory over *all* nations. Psalm 102:15, for example, predicts that "The nations will fear the name of the Lord and *all* kings of the earth thy glory."

This prophetic message is naturally repeated in the prophetic books. In the second chapter of Isaiah, for

102

example, we read that *all* nations and peoples shall flow to the house of the Lord in order to learn his ways and walk in them, that is, to become his disciples.

A beautiful summary statement of this major thread running through the Old Testament is found in Isaiah 45:22 which says, "Turn to me and be saved, *all* ends of the earth! For I am God, and there is no other."

The New Testament command

When we turn to the New Testament, the promise and vision of the future becomes an explicit command for the present. All four Gospels as well as the first chapter of Acts record our risen Lord's marching orders for his people from that time until his return: "Go and make disciples of *all* nations."

A number of the 12 disciples and the Apostle Paul are then seen in the process of obeying this command. In giving his testimony before King Agrippa, for example, Paul makes clear that his mission in life was to go to the nations (Gentiles) in order that these nations "may turn from darkness to light and from the power of Satan to God, that they may receive forgiveness of sins" (Acts 26:16-18).

Paul stresses this again in his concluding remarks to the Christians at Rome when he writes of making known the gospel to *all* nations according to the command of the living God that they might be brought to the obedience of faith (Rom. 16:26).

Before the close of the New Testament we again have this comprehensive view of the future when "*All* nations shall come and worship thee, for thy judgments have been revealed" (Rev. 15:4).

We also have great summary statements of the Lord's all-inclusiveness such as that expressed in 2 Peter 3:9: "The Lord is not slow about his promise as some count slowness, but is forbearing toward you, not wishing that *any* should perish, but that *all* should reach repentance."

It is this comprehensive purpose of the Lord that drives

us to the mobilization of the whole body of Christ in all nations to work most directly towards world evangelization. It is why we suggest a goal of 7 million more congregations. The Lord desires that *all* nations be brought to the obedience of faith and that *all* people should reach repentance.

In its emphasis on the discipling of *whole* nations and of *all* nations, DAWN is taking seriously this comprehensive purpose and plan of the Lord. It is therefore believed that this third ingredient of the DAWN concept is another powerful component in a strategy for the discipling of the nations.

4. DAWN IS BASED ON BIBLICAL MODELS OF THE *SYSTEMATIC* OCCUPATION OF THE LAND.

Not only do we need a comprehensive plan for all peoples, but we need a systematic approach so that no people group will be overlooked. At harvest time, the wheat farmer does not stroll willy-nilly through his fields, grabbing a few stalks of grain here and a few more there. Rather, he sets his combines or organizes his field workers so that every square foot is reaped.

The Joshua model

The Bible is not without evidence of such systematic planning. As I have spent these last three decades searching for a strategy for world evangelization, I have come to see that an Old Testament model for making "disciples of all nations" can be found in the Joshua account of possessing the land. This account was also, it seems to me, "written for our instruction, that by steadfastness and by the encouragement of the scriptures, we might have hope" (Rom. 15:4) in the task of making disciples of all nations.

In giving us his final command, the Lord left us a pattern to be studied, fathomed and applied to the primary task given us before his ascension. From this example we

104

can have hope, we can "be strong and of good courage," neither "frightened" nor "dismayed," as we enter more fully into the awesome task of making disciples of all peoples of the earth.

Among many other things suggested in Joshua's conquering the land of Canaan is this idea of a systematic approach. It is seen that every place the sole of his foot was to tread upon was to be his.

Taking possession of the land began with the exhilarating "battle" at Jericho. Next, Joshua sent his armies — after some difficult lessons had been learned — to the nearby tribe of Ai.

The Gibeonites (Joshua 9) and then the five kings of the Amorites (Joshua 10), seeing this step-by-step pattern, realized they were next to be conquered. The Gibeonites used trickery to avoid defeat, and the five kings attempted to forestall the inevitable by attacking first, though it turned out to be futile. After killing the kings at the cave of Makkedah, Joshua first took the tribe of Makkedah and then went on to conquer each of the five cities of the fallen kings.

In chapter 11 we see him similarly going out and systematically destroying kingdom after kingdom. All the kingdoms that had been conquered to date are then listed in specific detail in chapter 12.

But the task was not complete. In chapter 13 the Lord makes another list, this time giving great detail concerning each piece of land that remained to be taken. There was nothing haphazard in the conquering and possession of the land the Lord had promised to the children of Israel. Joshua was not to rest until absolutely every kingdom was captured and occupied.

Going to every village

Turning to the New Testament, we see in the first place that the ministry of John the Baptist, while centering in one area, still resulted in direct, personal contact with representatives from every locality as people came to him from "Jerusalem, and *all* Judea and *all* the region of Jordan" (Mt. 3:4-6).

Of Jesus it is recorded several times that he "went about *all* the cities and villages, teaching in their synagogues and preaching the gospel of the kingdom, healing every disease and infirmity" in Galilee (Mt. 9:35). According to Josephus, this included 204 villages with an average of 15,000 people. To accomplish such a project certainly implies systematic planning and implementation.

The Apostle Paul used this same systematic approach of either going personally to every local area or seeing that his ministry extended to each such area.

In Acts 13:4-6 we see him at the beginning of his ministry going with Barnabas through the *whole* island of Cyprus beginning at Salamis on one end and finishing at Paphos on the other. Later we read (Acts 19:8-10) that Paul spent two years teaching *all* who passed through Ephesus with the result that they took the gospel with them "so that *all* the residents of Asia heard the word of the Lord, both Jews and Greeks."

Philip had a similarly systematic ministry after being taken by the Spirit to lead the Ethiopian eunuch to Christ. After the Ethiopian went on his way, it says that "Philip was found at Azotus, and passing on he preached the gospel to *all* the towns till he came to Caesarea" (Acts 8:40).

The fourth powerful ingredient of the DAWN approach is that it follows the models of Joshua, John the Baptist, Jesus, Paul and other apostles as they systematically went about possessing the land. It takes literally the command to "disciple all the nations" by developing a practical, systematic plan for accomplishing this task.

How DAWN is put together in a comprehensive and systematic plan will be further explained as we go along.

"The way I run my business"

It is this systematic and comprehensive approach, by the way, that seems to give DAWN much of its appeal. "I like DAWN because that's the way I run my business," said a wealthy businessman who plans to introduce DAWN in his native Norway.

We hear such comments quite frequently. Ian Robertson could also see the connection to his business. He is a top-level consultant for Lockheed who gives seminars on the manufacturing process. "DAWN is the only missions strategy I know of that works on the systems level," he says. "Every other strategy emphasizes one aspect, but no one else sees the whole picture like DAWN does."

He explained this from the manufacturing process. "There are some who are expert in research, some in product development, some in the actual manufacturing, some in sales, some in administration. Each is isolated in his or her own specialty. But very few see the whole process or how the whole system functions. Churches and missions are in the same situation. But DAWN works at this systems level."

5. DAWN IS BUILT ON THE PRACTICAL AND EMOTIONAL VALUES OF A "WHOLE-COUNTRY" APPROACH.

In developing a comprehensive and systematic approach to the completion of the Great Commission, it is necessary to divide the task into manageable segments. On the one hand we have the whole body of Christ in the world consisting of about 330 to 400 million believers, the "harvest force." On the other hand, we have all the nations of the world that need to be discipled, the "harvest field."

Can we break up the "harvest force" and the "harvest field" into such manageable segments that the whole body of Christ in the whole world will so be put to work that no part of the harvest field will be neglected?

The simplest, most direct way to do this, I have concluded after many years, is with a country-by-country approach. Dividing all the "nations" and all the believers of the world by countries is the only practical, workable way of making sure that *every* "nation" is going to be reached.

The exploded myth

At first blush, this might sound anachronistic. Haven't the missiologists of our day exploded the myth that the "nations" Jesus refers to in his final command are not the same as the geopolitical entities we call "countries" today? Haven't they made it clear that each people group within a country needs its own evangelistic approach?

Yes, they have.

But countries are also a world reality. The world is conveniently divided into something like 223 geopolitical entities that have a great number of factors that tend to unify them. Barrett, for example, lists 25 shared characteristics held in common by the people of a country.

As Ed Dayton wrote in a letter to me, "There is little doubt but that we are forced to look at the world in terms of political boundaries — nation states. Not to consider it this way would be not only poor strategy but poor missiology."

Dayton also wrote that "The only way to come up with a statistical analysis of the world is in terms of nation-states. These are the buckets into which we have to fit people."

This division by countries is how the world system operates. There is little to be gained by ignoring it.

Countries are a missions and Church reality as well. Most societies and denominations divide their work by countries. The most practical way to divide the body of Christ in the world for a real attempt at completing the Great Commission, then, is through the structure that is already in place.

Dividing the people groups of the world by countries is the only practical way to reach them *all*. By some definitions of the biblical term "nation" there are about 9,000 such groups in the world. By other definitions there are about 16,000 unreached people groups alone. By other definitions there may be as many as 100,000 or even many more people groups in the world. If we are to work effectively and systematically at making disciples of *all* the "nations" of the world, we must find a practical way of dividing them into manageable segments. The country approach does just that.

As Wade Coggins of EFMA says, "There are practical things about a country that are still viable. 'Countryhood' still has something to say to us with regard to the task. Our new perception of the world composed of thousands of people groups doesn't mean we should abandon other perceptions of the world. Wedding the two ideas is really the way to go."

Ralph Winter suggests a similar strategy. His idea was to have a center for world mission in every possible country in the world. Such centers would have a two-fold vision. They would look outward to see what unreached people groups there were in the world to whom they might send missionaries. But they would also look inward to their own country to see what unreached people groups remained to be discipled. So Winter's strategy for entering the vast array of hidden peoples has a country focus at the heart of it.

Dividing the people groups of the world by countries is the only practical way to work towards the *discipling* of each group. By working at the goal of an evangelical congregation in every small village and neighborhood of a whole country, we are automatically working most directly at the very complicated task of making disciples of all peoples. In the process of thus saturating a country with churches, every people group is likewise being saturated with cells of believers.

The power of patriotism

The above are the practical aspects. But there is the emotional side as well.

Most people feel a great sense of patriotism and love of country, perhaps believers even more. In reporting on a national missions conference held in Guatemala a few years ago, Wade Coggins spoke of the "enormous insistence that they were Guatemalans and ought to be doing something about reaching all the peoples in their country. There was this tremendous feeling of national pride and putting themselves on the line for reaching their whole country."

In attending various international conferences, I personally have observed, in the patriotic songs sung, in the wearing of national dress and in the references to native lands, a great sense of pride and love for the homeland.

Even in South Africa I found this same love of homeland whether I was among whites of British descent, whites of Dutch descent, blacks of various tribes, Indians or coloreds. There were problems with the system, but love for the mother country.

Missions, revival and evangelism history is full of men who had this tremendous love for country. Such a one was John Knox who spoke and lived by the cry of "Give me Scotland or I die." He emulated such men as Nehemiah who mourned, wept, fasted and prayed for his native Jerusalem; as Jesus who wept over the same city and longed to gather it under his protection as a hen gathers her brood; as the Apostle Paul who went so far as to wish that he "were accursed and cut off from Christ for the sake of my brethren, my kinsmen by race" (Rom. 9:3).

This love for one's native country along with the practical realities of countryhood and mission structure, then, is a fifth powerful ingredient in the DAWN approach. Dividing the world by countries gives us manageable segments for working systematically at the comprehensive task of the Great Commission.

Chapter summary

By way of summary, the first five components of the DAWN strategy that seem to make it a powerful force for world evangelization are its Christ-centeredness, its focus on the most effective evangelistic method, its comprehensive viewpoint, its systematic approach and its division of the total task into practical and manageable segments.

Ingredient number six is so significant that we will take our longest chapter for its presentation.

Chapter 9

The Power of Information

As indicated, I want to spend a little more time on the next powerful ingredient of the DAWN process. Of the 12 components of DAWN, this one is first among equals. It is at the same time the ingredient least understood, most often maligned and in some respects most difficult and expensive to accomplish. But without this step there simply will not be a DAWN project, and probably no commitment to significant national goals nor to the worldwide goal of 7 million more churches. It concerns the matter of research. This is the next basic concept in the DAWN process:

6. DAWN RELEASES THE INCREDIBLE POWER OF INFORMATION.

My negative experiences with the idea of research can be rolled up in one incident. A few years ago a close friend related to me the comment of a key missions committee member of a large church. "We have a million dollar budget for missions," he boasted, "and not one penny for research."

He was bragging! He was insisting! As long as he was

on the missions committee, not one penny would be "wasted" on research.

The transformation of William Carey

When I come across such derogatory comments about research, I find comfort in the work of William Carey, surely one who would be acceptable among members of most missions committees. Even the lengthy title of his most famous pamphlet endorsed such an activity:

An
ENQUIRY
into the
OBLIGATIONS OF CHRISTIANS
to use means for the
CONVERSION
of the
HEATHENS.

In which the
Religious State of the Different Nations
of the World, the Success of Former
Undertakings, and the practicability of
Further Undertakings, are Considered.

The second part of this title, by the way, includes three basic aspects of DAWN research that will be discussed further: gathering *contextual* data ("Religious State of the nations"), gathering *institutional* data ("Success of Former Undertakings") and the *prophetic message* emerging from data ("Practicability of Further Undertakings").

What drove Carey to compile the data and write the book, however, is at the heart of our present concern for doing research. It was to arouse his generation in England to the need for making disciples of the peoples of the world.

According to Deaville Walker, one of Carey's biographers, Carey himself had been awakened to his missionary calling through the gathering of information, another way to speak of "research." When his own heart had been broken by what he had learned of the the vast needs of people especially in the South Sea Islands, he began to challenge his fellow ministers with his growing missionary vision.

Finally came the historic meeting when Carey, as a young man, attended a ministers' meeting in Northampton, England, in 1786. Toward the end of the meeting, the famous preacher, Dr. John Collett Ryland, invited the young men present to propose a topic for general discussion. With some hesitation, according to Walker, Carey rose and suggested that the group discuss:

> Whether the command given to the Apostles to teach all nations was not obligatory on all succeeding ministers to the end of the world, seeing that the accompanying promise was of equal extent.[1]

"Carey's suggestion," writes Walker, "stunned all those present. Dr. Ryland immediately declared his idea to be absurd. 'Young man,' he exclaimed, 'sit down: when God pleases to convert the heathen, he will do it without your aid or mine!'

"Carey sat down — disappointed but not discouraged," Walker continues, "for he was sure of his ground. He had read books Dr. Ryland had not read; and he realized what his senior colleagues did not — the depth of human need. He was silenced for the moment, but only for the moment. He saw that *his first task must be to pass on to others the information that had stirred his own heart; he must transmit to them his vision*" (emphasis mine).[2]

His vision that was aroused through the data he had gathered would ultimately launch the modern missionary era in the publishing of his ENQUIRY, an 87-page booklet written by Carey at the age of 31 in 1792. Of this memorable document, Walker says:

This remarkable pamphlet was one of the greatest achievements of Carey's career, and an important landmark of modern missions. It was in every way unique. . . . Carey's pamphlet was a reasoned statement of Christian obligation, of world needs, of existing opportunities, and practical proposals for the formation of a missionary society. . . . So far as our knowledge goes, no one, through all the centuries of the Christian era, had made so careful and systematic a survey of human needs and missionary opportunities as that self-taught peasant, and even today we read with amazement the product of his indefatigable industry and heart passion.[3]

Carey launched the modern missions movement because of the information he had gathered "that had stirred his own heart." He realized he had to pass on this information and thereby transmit his vision.

This is why we make data gathering such a prime concern in DAWN. It is why we say "DAWN releases the incredible power of information."

The Nehemiah Effect

This is also what we refer to as the "the Nehemiah Effect." In the opening sessions of seminars on missionary research, I frequently ask the following series of questions:

What was it that caused Nehemiah — who had never before been sad in the presence of the king — to begin a period of mourning and weeping and fasting and praying over a number of months?

What brought his attention to his sins, the sins of his father's house and the sins of the people of Israel, and to confess them with a broken heart?

Why would he go to the king with a request that could cost him his life if it displeased the king?

Why would he give up the good life in the vacation, political and economic center of the world for the dangerous

116

journey across the desert to Jerusalem?

What could possibly motivate him to go to the obviously discouraged people of Israel who were content — or at least resigned — to live in the rubble their city had become?

Why would he give up everything to attempt such a depressing task that would only arouse the surrounding enemies to ridicule, deceit and even armed attack?

If we can find the answers to these questions, I believe we can find at least part of the answer to how we can get a fragmented, weak, national Church with a low self-image to rally around the task of filling its nation with expressions of the powerful, living Christ in every small segment of every rural village and city neighborhood.

The answers I get in the seminars are usually of a good, spiritual nature with truth in them. But they rarely get back to the starting point. This whole incredible sequence of events began for Nehemiah when he was presented with some information.

He learned that the survivors of the devastated city of Jerusalem were in great shame and trouble. The gates and the walls were broken down and the peoples round about were mocking them and their God.

That's what brought it all about. As would be true of William Carey, once Nehemiah was faced with the reality of the situation, there was kindled a fire in his bones. He could not but give of himself — at whatever the cost — to attempt the restoration of the city of God.

Let us rise up and build

Nehemiah not only had his own life immeasurably transformed by information, but he used this "incredibly powerful tool" to transform the Jerusalem rabble as well. For after going out secretly by night to survey the situation, he gathered "the Jews, the priests, the nobles, the officials, and the rest" and said to them:

You see the trouble we are in, how Jerusalem lies

117

in ruins with its gates burned [contextual data].
Come let us build the wall of Jerusalem, that we
may no longer suffer disgrace [the prophetic
message] (Neh. 2:17).

He gave them further information concerning God's
hand upon him (institutional data) and also the encouraging words of the king.

The dramatic effect was to stiffen the spine, strengthen
the hands, enlarge the heart and vision of this discouraged
and disorganized rabble to the unanimous cry: "Let us rise
up and build" (2:18).

And that they did despite every subtle and frontal
attack of surrounding enemies without and troublemakers
within.

How can we similarly get Christian leaders and workers to toss everything familiar, comfortable, habitual and
of great value to them to embark on a project that likewise
appears impossible and doomed to failure and disgrace
from the beginning? How can the Church of a nation be
effectively mobilized to make a realistic attempt at the
discipling of its nation?

That is one of the tasks of research. It is to so gather
and so present information that the people of God will be
moved to do more effectively the work of God.

Seen in this light, research really is not so bad after
all, is it?

The Nehemiah Effect in Silicon Valley

I've seen this "Nehemiah Effect" strike often and
strike hard.

It happened, for example, in 1985 in Santa Clara
County, better known worldwide as Silicon Valley.

Though the area had produced a number of "super
churches" that had grown from a handful of people into
congregations numbering into the thousands, the overall
evangelistic picture had not been that great.

As one pastor put it, "Every five or ten years a few evangelical leaders start feeling guilty about our lack of evangelism. So they get together and ask, 'Should we invite Luis or Billy?' A crusade is held, and then the Church rests for another five or ten years when the process is repeated."

The lament was not aimed at city-wide crusades, but the lack of an effective, continuous program of outreach by a majority of the churches of the area.

In chapter four we mentioned the RISE Santa Clara County organization that determined to do something about the situation. Through its first research project it was discovered that in this valley of mega churches and 24-hour Christian TV stations only 6.8 percent of the entire population could be found in a protestant church of any kind on a Sunday morning! This broke down to 8.6 percent among Anglos but just 4 percent for ethnics.

We have seen that among the 40 percent of the population that was non-Anglo, the situation was particularly bad. For the county's 300,000 Hispanics, there were only 45 mostly tiny churches with a total of 3,475 members, barely 1.2 percent of their community.

There were *no* churches for 930 Afghans, 8,506 American Indians, 6,000 Asian Indians, 566 East Europeans, 2,320 Ethiopians, 1,563 Guamanians, 1,608 Hawaiians, 4,000 Iranians and 617 Iraqis.

When a group of about 100 area pastors gathered for a report on this research, the Nehemiah Effect took hold:

"Shocking!" exclaimed one San Jose pastor.

"I was crushed," said another. "I fell on my face in prayer."

"I had no idea of the size of the mission field right here," said still another.

So stirred were these pastors that they agreed to a hold a congress sponsored by RISE in order to determine what should be done. Several months later, many of these same pastors came forward at the congress to affix their signatures to a document that proclaimed the intention of the Church of Santa Clara County to increase from about 85,000 in average attendance to 300,000 by the year AD 2000.

Furthermore, the air was filled with loud "amens" when one leader suggested they should develop the project so effectively that the RISE movement would spread throughout the whole country with the purpose of dis-cipling the U.S. in our time.

Whether, like Nehemiah, this group will persevere with the project over the coming years and see it spread throughout the nation remains to be seen. But for now it is another striking example of the power of information to move men and women of God to greater vision and endeavor.

The "Effect" around the world

The "Nehemiah Effect" did its work in Zaire at a con-gress in 1985. "For 50 years," says missionary Willys Braun, "the Church here has been content that what had been known as the 'Belgian Congo' had become a Christian nation. The Church could now busy itself with other worthwhile activities."

Then, in a DAWN-type national congress in 1985, Braun challenged some 300 leaders with the *real* situation: This "Christian" nation had about 60,000 villages but only 10,000 village churches. At least 50,000 villages had no resident Christian witness at all! In the cities, there was only one evangelical church for every 10,000 people!

So alarmed were these leaders by the "trouble and shame" of their situation that they made commitment to plant another 10,000 village churches and 5,000 city churches in the next five years. When this would be accomplished, more than a million new converts would be attending evangelical churches. One Church after another got busy with this project.

In his Evangelism/Church Growth seminars held in more than 50 countries in the 1970s, Vergil Gerber repeat-edly observed this phenomenon. Delegates were required to bring with them statistical data of their churches for the previous 11 years. When they analyzed their own graphs and rates of growth, they responded almost invariably with a great new vision of how much more they could accomplish for the Lord. Again and again the incredible power of information did its work.

I observed this personally in the workshop held with Gerber, McGavran and a few others in the Philippines in 1974. It was in this session that denominational leaders studied not only their own data and that of others, but some simple observations about the country as a whole.

It was when the information gathered about the great potential responsiveness of the people was presented, along with the mathematical reality that the number of churches could explode from the current 5,000 to 50,000 by the end of the century, that the 75 leaders as one committed themselves to this goal.

Except on the island of Mindanao, there was very little follow-up on a national level to this commitment. Yet in gathering data four years later, it was found that many denominations had gone back to their own groups, set their own goals, developed their own programs *and were now growing at a rate twice as fast as they had in the previous decade!*

It is now 14 years later and the Church of the whole country is keeping up this pace and is more committed than ever to the goal.

Positive data as well as negative data — as in the cases of Nehemiah and Silicon Valley — can motivate a Church to greater evangelistic and church-planting zeal.

For example, in 1984 a group of about 350 evangelical leaders in Guatemala saw not so much the trouble they were in as the excellent growth and great opportunity their situation afforded. They made a commitment to see their nation become at least 50 percent evangelical by the end of 1990. It would make them the first majority evangelical nation in Latin America and perhaps the whole world.

Data gathered by Roy Wingerd of Overseas Crusades

121

indicates "a whole new wave of evangelism and church planting" as one leader expressed it. One denomination, for example, had been adding about 4,000 converts a year to their church rolls. In the year after the DAWN-type congress, however, they added 10,000 newly converted members! In all there are 15 denominations that have developed growth programs. If these groups alone reach their goals, the country will be more than 50 percent evangelical by their target date, according to Wingerd.

Similarly, when the Conservative Baptists in the Philippines were a tiny group of 21 churches and 1,500 members in 1970, Leonard Tuggy pointed out to them that, though small, they were growing at a very good average annual rate of 20 percent. Then Tuggy showed the group what would happen if they continued at that growth rate for another ten years — a most difficult task since it is quite a bit easier to grow rapidly when small than when getting larger.

It was seen that within a decade they could explode up to 200 churches and 10,000 members.

"Why don't we launch 'Operation 200'" someone said. They did. A decade later they had topped their goal of 10,000 members and come close to the goal of 200 churches. This achievement paved the way for "Harvest 20,000" which in turn prompted the current goal of 90,000 members by 1990.

And it all began with a simple presentation and analysis of their growth data. The tens of thousands they are winning to Christ and bringing into their multiplying number of churches *above that which could have been expected from a more "normal" or average rate of growth* is testimony again to the tremendous power of information.

Biblical insights on research

With this empirical data about the power of information, it is not surprising to look into the scriptures and find what we do.

Nehemiah, of course, not only received his initial vision through the information presented, but once back in Jerusalem he began a second level of research. He went out by night with a few trusted men for an inspection tour of the walls and the gates. He needed to know the extent of the damage, the materials that would be necessary and an idea of the work force that would be required (Neh. 2:11-16).

This is a reminder of the words of the Lord when he asked: "For which of you, desiring to build a tower, does not first sit down and count the cost, whether he has enough to complete it? . . . Or what king, going to encounter another king in war, will not sit down first to take counsel whether he is able with ten thousand to meet him who comes against him with twenty thousand?"

It is only natural, says the Lord with these rhetorical questions, to gather information before embarking on a project to determine ahead of time whether or not the project can be successfully completed. Is not the Great Commission "project" worthy of this attention as well?

The book of Proverbs is full of admonitions to gather the facts beforehand. The Living Bible translation makes these especially pointed:

"Plans go wrong with too few counselors; many counselors bring success" (15:22). Presumably, the more counselors there are, the more information is brought to bear on the subject.

"The intelligent man is always open to new ideas. In fact, he looks for them" (18:15). Looking for new ideas is certainly one aspect of what we can call "research."

"The wise man thinks ahead; a fool doesn't, and even brags about it!" (13:16). No comment needed.

And here's the one that speaks most sharply: "What a shame — yes, how stupid! — to decide before knowing the facts!" (18:13).

Not only does the Bible challenge us to seek facts and gather information, it shows the Lord himself doing research. John Robb, a senior researcher at MARC, points out that 2 Chronicles 16:9 speaks of the Lord continuing to

123

survey the earth and its inhabitants in an ongoing way till the end of time: "For the eyes of the Lord run to and fro throughout the whole earth to show his might in behalf of those whose heart is blameless towards him."[4]

Robb also notes that in Ezekiel 20:6, God speaks of bringing Israel out of Egypt "into a land I had searched out for them, a land flowing with milk and honey."

When we look to the Old Testament metaphor for the discipling of a nation — that of Joshua possessing the land of Canaan — we see that the conquering of the land was not devoid of data gathering or what we might call "research." There were such activities as numbering, spying, observing, interviewing, listening and recording. These all related to the gathering of data for the task of possessing the land.

A study of Joshua reveals a further complexity to the biblical and church growth task of research. Among other things, I see four purposes and four pitfalls of research.

Four Purposes of Research

1. Gather "institutional" data about our resources for the discipling of nations.

Long before the children of Israel approached the promised land, the men of every tribe and family and household, "every male from twenty years and upward, all who were able to go forth to war," were carefully counted. Moses and Aaron were making an accurate inventory of their military resources before beginning the campaign to conquer all of Canaan.

When this is applied to Great Commission thinking, we have come to call this "institutional" research. That is, we look at the resources within the "institution" of the Church in light of the task of the Great Commission.

In a nationwide survey, this can include making a list of all denominations according to their tradition, determining their geographical scope and sociological emphasis, finding their total number of congregations and total communicant members, establishing their Average Annual Growth Rates (AAGR's) over the period of their histories, digging out the various factors that account for their slow or rapid growth and so on. When this data is collated and analyzed for the Church of a whole nation, a fairly accurate picture emerges as to the potential the Church has for an aggressive attempt at discipling the whole nation.

2. Gather "contextual" data that relates to the discipling of nations.

This is modeled for us in Numbers 13:1 and 17-20. The Lord told Moses to "Send men to spy out the land of Canaan, which I give to the people of Israel; from each tribe of their fathers shall you send a man, every one a leader among them."

When these men had been chosen, Moses gave them their research plan. "Go up into the Negeb yonder, and go up into the hill country," he said, "and see what the land is, and whether the people who dwell in it are strong or weak, whether they are few or many, and whether the land that they dwell in is good or bad, and whether the cities that they dwell in are camps or strongholds, and whether the land is rich or poor, and whether there is wood in it or not. Be of good courage, and bring some of the fruit of the land."

These instructions indicate they were to gather information relating to the coming battles against the Canaanites, the availability of supplies to support the invaders and the value of the land they would eventually occupy.

Gathering information about the resources Moses had within the people of Israel we called "institutional" data. Gathering information about the peoples to be conquered we refer to as "contextual" data. "Institutional" information referred to everything that could be learned about what was inside the nation of Israel. "Contextual" information, then, refers to everything outside.

The parallel to our situation is clear. "Institutional" data refers to everything we can learn about the size,

growth rates, effective methodologies, strengths and resources of the Church for the task of the Great Commission
in a nation. "Contextual" data refers to everything outside
the Church, or the "context" of the Church. Waymire's
terminology is again helpful as he refers to the "harvest
force" — the Church — and the "harvest field" — everything and everybody in society outside the Church.

More specifically, contextual data refers to information
about the culture, history, economy, politics, sociology,
religion and other societal factors that have bearing on the
discipling of a nation. Two matters in particular that have
such bearing are covered in the next two purposes.

**3. Determine responsiveness to the gospel from the
contextual data.**

When Joshua sent his researchers/spies to Jericho there
was one dominant impression they came away with: "Truly
the Lord has given all the land into our hands;" they
reported to Joshua, "and moreover all the inhabitants of
the land are fainthearted because of us" (Joshua 2:24).
They had come to this conclusion in part, no doubt, from
their observations. But there was also the interview with
Rahab, the harlot. She and all the people of Jericho had
heard of the parting of the Red Sea and of the utter
destruction of Sihon and Og, the Amorite kings.

"I know that the Lord has given you the land," she told
them, "and that the fear of you has fallen upon us, and that
all the inhabitants of the land melt away before you."

If ever there were a kingdom ready to be captured, this
was it. They were totally demoralized and had mentally
accepted their eventual defeat.

This was not the situation at Ai, by the way. The
armies there were ready for battle, and in fact sent the
Israelites back with their first casualties and first defeat.

These examples of the relative readiness of a people to
accept defeat on literal battle fields in the Old Testament
speak to me of the New Testament concept of "harvest" or
readiness to accept the gospel. There are times when an

individual or a family, a segment of a population or even a whole people group — and sometimes a whole country! — is more open to change and therefore to the gospel than they would be at other times or places.

A selective study of various societal factors that make up the context of the Church can reveal much information about potential responsiveness. With a clearer idea of just how ready a people is to accept the gospel, the Church can move forward with more confidence and boldness (or even audacity as we see in the battle plan for Jericho) in the discipling of a nation.

4. Determine the methodologies that will be most productive in bringing the maximum number of the unsaved to Christ and active participation in his Church.

These methodologies can be found both from a look at the context and a look at the institution.

Referring to the Joshua model again, we find there was a variety of methodologies used for the conquering of nations or city/states in the land of Canaan.

At Jericho, where the people were ready to capitulate, the Lord led Joshua to a methodology that frightened the inhabitants still further by simply marching around the walls once a day for six days and seven times the seventh day.

Again, perhaps thinking Ai would be as easy to take as Jericho, a small band of warriors marched right into their first defeat. Now it was the Israelites whose hearts "melted, and became as water" (7:5). When they later settled the problem of sin in the camp, they went back with a strategy appropriate for this situation. That is, they lured the enemy into an ambush that had been set for them and utterly defeated them.

On another occasion, the king of Jerusalem decided not to await the forces of Joshua, but to band together with four other kings and attack them (chapter 10). This "contextual" factor called for a different strategy. On this occasion, Joshua called for an all-night forced march so that they came upon the enemies at Gibeon suddenly and threw them into a panic. The result was a great slaughter and mighty victory for Israel.

After this there followed a new methodology that became the basic strategy for a number of nations. This is pictured for us in chapter 10 where over and over it says that Joshua passed on with all Israel to a certain city, laid siege to it and/or assaulted it, and took it on that day, and smote it with the edge of the sword and utterly destroyed every person in it.

The first group of battles mentioned above was characterized by a different strategy or method for each situation. These differing strategies were suggested by the differing circumstances. In the second group, the same basic strategy was used over and over.

Similarly, a careful study of the context of the Church — whether it be on a local, regional, people group or national basis — will suggest what methodologies will be most productive in the disciple-making process. Such successful methodologies will be discovered as the researcher asks church leaders what has accounted for their rapid growth — when such growth is found.

To summarize, the Joshua model illustrates these four purposes of research: understanding the institution of the Church, understanding the context of the Church, determining potential responsiveness to the gospel and determining most effective evangelistic methodologies.

These purposes of research, however, must be kept in perspective with the other side of the coin, the pitfalls of research.

The four pitfalls in research

1. Gathering data for prideful, sinful purposes.

The four purposes for research we have been sharing all deal with our effectiveness, our good stewardship, in carrying out the command of the Lord to make disciples of all peoples. In this respect, data gathering becomes an aid, a tool for accomplishing the task.

But an instrument can be used for good or for evil. On two occasions, for example, Moses counted his warriors. These were the occasions of leaving Egypt when Moses expected he would immediately enter the promised land to take possession of it, and 40 years later when they were actually to cross the Jordan and begin the military campaigns. This numbering of his troops would be a normal function for a commander going forth to war, and was not sinful nor punished by the Lord.

But on another occasion (recorded in 2 Samuel 24), King David, against the counsel of Joab, his military commander, sent out his army commanders in a ten-month task of counting his military forces. When the task was completed, however, David's heart was smitten with guilt. He confessed his sin and was given three options for his punishment.

In this case, the numbering of his valiant men who drew the sword was not for strategic planning, but for pride, "to please himself with the exhibition of the imposing military strength of his people," according to one commentator.

If even David could fall into this sin, surely we are capable of it as well. So all churches, pastors, denomination leaders or researchers must guard themselves against counting their people, determining their growth rates or comparing their "success" with those of others merely to massage their own egos. Not only is it sin, but it will lead them to the wrong conclusions and therefore wrong strategies as well, as we will see in the next pitfall.

2. Misinterpreting the data.

This is a problem perhaps worse than getting no data at all. We know that figures don't lie, but that liars figure. We can make data say almost anything we want. If we approach data with preconceived ideas, prejudices, pride or simply poor judgment, we will come to the wrong conclusions about them every time.

We see this illustrated for us again in the story of

Moses sending in the 12 "researchers" to spy out the land. Using the exact same data, two of them came to the right conclusion, but 10 of them came to the more popular conclusion which was to cost all the adults a 40-year sentence in the desert and a loss of the opportunity to enter the promised land. *That's* how important a correct interpretation of the data is.

This task is more a skill, an art and a spiritual exercise than gathering the information itself. If we approach data with our fears and unbelief, we will come to the wrong conclusions, take wrong actions and miss the tremendous blessing and victory the Lord has in store for us.

"Rightly dividing" the data is almost as crucial as "rightly dividing" the Word itself. When all the information is gathered about the institution and context of the Church, the deeply spiritual, exceedingly important task of interpreting the data is begun. When this exercise is correctly handled, a prophetic message to the Church begins to emerge.

3. Overreliance on data.

One of the factors that contributed to the demoralizing defeat at Ai (Joshua 7) was an overzealous belief in the information they had found. With their easy victory at Jericho, it could well be they approached their spying with some preconceived ideas and perhaps a less than thorough research job. Then they went on to the disastrous conclusion that they could take this city with a token force. Their data was quite likely faulty in the first place and they compounded this problem by relying too heavily on it.

If they had done further "institutional" research, they might have uncovered the sin that was in the camp and realized that despite the objective evidence, there could be no easy victory.

No, information gathering, research, evaluating the data cannot serve as a *substitute* for righteousness and spiritual dynamic in the Church. A strong discipleship training program, prayer, revival and confession of sin must go hand in hand with a strong evangelism program based at least in part on what we learn from our context and our institution.

4. Making decisions with incomplete data.

When it came time to deal with the Gibeonites (Joshua 9), the interview method of "research" was used. The Gibeonites came with the claim and apparently objective evidence that they had come from a far country. (The fact that they came with stale bread and worn sandals indicates they *expected* Joshua to do some research about them.)

Joshua questioned them, asking if they didn't really live among them, asking who they were and where they had come from. Joshua accepted the answers and evidence at face value without further corroboration. They didn't get *enough* information either from the Gibeonites or from the Lord as "they did not ask direction from the Lord" (vs. 14).

Using the interview method of research in dealing with the Gibeonites was not a bad idea in itself. But they quit too soon, before they learned how they had been deceived. With a more in-depth study, they might have saved themselves a lot of grief during their time and in succeeding generations.

Of course, it is possible to gather too much data. I am familiar, for instance, with criticisms of some church growth researchers who "count telephone poles." (There were approximately 100,000 in Manila in 1975.) But conclusions arrived at with too little information can be as disastrous as no information or misinterpretation of the information.

The wind of the Spirit

By now I trust the reader has a good feeling about the task of research as it relates to completing the Great Commission. Gathering enough of the right kind of data and giving it careful analysis and interpretation can be an immense help in the task of making disciples of all nations. Under various names, research is taught in the Word, it is modeled and carried out by the Lord himself and it has a great track record in actual practice. It is a biblical concept and it is a powerful tool. For Joshua's military campaign as well as for the spiritual warfare inherent in working at completing the Great Commission there is the need for intelligence, for information, for sufficient, accurate, carefully and prayerfully analyzed data both for the institution and the context of the Church.

One final word. In my mind, this type of church growth research can be boiled down to the simple need to know and understand how the wind of the Spirit is blowing over both the society and the Church in order to enhance our effectiveness in regard to our evangelistic mandate. From this understanding we can then get a more accurate picture of what the Spirit would want to accomplish through his Church in the succeeding months and years.

This is what we refer to as the "prophetic message" that emerges from the gathering and analysis of data and is the next powerful ingredient of the DAWN process.

Notes

1. Deaville F. Walker, *William Carey: Missionary Pioneer and Statesman,* (Chicago: Moody Press, 1960), p. 49.
2. Ibid., p. 54.
3. Ibid., pp. 67-68.
4. John Robb, "Survey and Possess the Land," *Frontier Missions,* July 1985, p. 198.

Chapter 10

The Prophetic Message

With that long explanation of the need for careful research, we now turn to a look at what we *do* with the data that has been collected. This is the next aspect of the DAWN strategy that makes it so powerful:

7. DAWN HELPS FIND THE PROPHETIC MESSAGE.

As we have seen, in gathering information for a DAWN project we generally look to both the "context" and "institution" of the Church to determine the work of the Spirit and the direction he is moving. From this it is then possible to develop a better understanding of where he wants to take the Church in the years immediately ahead.

This is what we call the "prophetic message." It is powerful not because it is an idea dreamed up in America and exported to other lands. Rather, it is a glimpse of a country and its Church from God's perspective. Analyzing and describing what is seen becomes God's voice which his people will hear and follow.

One role of the prophet is to communicate vision, a picture of what can happen, of what ought to happen, of what God wants to happen. Without such a vision, "the people perish;" but with a clear vision of what God wants to accomplish, people's hearts are fired.

This prophetic message is the goal of the researcher's efforts. Data is gathered not to fill books that sit on shelves, but to be analyzed and understood. From this analysis, along with all the teaching of the Word, fervent prayer and solid missiology, comes the message to the Church in terms of the next step it must take to work seriously at the command to disciple its nation.

The context in Guatemala

A quick look at our Guatemala experience illustrates the point.

In studying the social, historical, religious, political, financial, racial and societal context of the Church in Guatemala, we found an abundance of factors that all pointed to the possibility of a population very responsive to the gospel.

It was akin to the discovery of the "researchers" sent into Jericho. They found a people whose hearts melted with fear and warriors from whom all courage had been drained. They had heard of the mighty works of God and the utter defeat of Sihon and Og and concluded they were the next to be crushed by God's armies.

The comparison is this: The people of Jericho were demoralized, ready to be conquered. The people of Guatemala, we found, were similarly demoralized by many of their circumstances and were therefore ready for change. Other factors in their society were not negative but still further contributed to their openness to change.

In missiological parlance this is called "responsiveness." The Word frequently speaks of this condition as being a time for harvest.

Some of the contextual factors were as follows:

134

Guatemala historically had been a nation in upheaval. The insurrections, the coups and counter-coups, the struggles between right and left had continued for centuries. The nation was in the throes of guerrilla/anti-guerrilla warfare with great numbers of citizens being killed by who knows whom.

In 1976 the countryside suffered a devastating earthquake that killed thousands, ruined whole villages, destroyed roads and industry and disrupted the whole economy. This came to a society that already had masses of poor people who were frustrated in seeking a better life.

It had been a Roman Catholic nation for centuries, and therefore, well familiar with some forms and terms of Christianity. But it was a Christianity that seemed helpless in meeting the heart needs of the people and dealing with the problems that continuously plagued the country.

Furthermore, in a concern over the political power of the Catholic Church, President Justo Rufino Barrios in 1873 proclaimed religious liberty for Guatemala and invited the Presbyterian Church to send missionaries. For more than a century, then, the power of the Roman Church over the people has been weakening and gradually less and less stigma has been attached to becoming an evangelical. The time had come when it was no longer necessary to be a Roman Catholic to be thought a good Guatemalan.

On top of all this was a country still 50 percent tribal with more than another 40 percent who were tribal in background. This Mayan presence and background with its animistic roots provided a fertile soil for a religion that was not only more powerful than theirs, but had the good of the people at heart as well.

This very favorable set of circumstances indicated a very high degree of potential responsiveness.

Was this not known?

But didn't the Guatemalan Christians know all this?

Yes and no. Yes, there had to be awareness of much or all of these circumstances.

But no, the Church as a whole had not necessarily put them all together and seen the hand of the Lord in them. They were matters of fact, or hardships to be endured; but were they circumstances the Lord had allowed for their greater ability to win the nation for Christ? Was it God the Holy Spirit brooding over the land and so working in society that many more might seek him out and find him? Were evangelicals seeing all this from the viewpoint of a Joseph who recognized that what had been meant for evil, God had meant for good that many might be saved alive (Gen. 50:20)?

Perhaps there were those who did. But there was also the need for a prophetic message that systematized this information, analyzed it and from it determined and proclaimed God's message.

Those living in Jerusalem in Nehemiah's time certainly were aware of their hard lot. But apparently no one from within the city perceived the significance of their situation. Here was the city of the most high, all-powerful God in ruins and held in derision by mere man. Only Nehemiah became enraged enough at this incongruity to take the bold steps necessary to change the situation.

Someone had to evaluate the situation from God's viewpoint and formulate the Lord's prophetic message from it.

Not all countries will be found in such a favorable situation for evangelism as Guatemala. The context of the Church in each country (as well as every region and portion of it) will be distinct.

So the prophetic message to the Church of one land will be different from another. What will be possible in one place will not be possible in another.

But this is precisely the power of the prophetic message in the DAWN strategy. What is being said to the believers of any particular nation is a message for them, drawn from their situation. It is what God is saying to his

136

people in a particular circumstance. It is real. It is relevant. It hits between the eyes.

Page two of the prophetic message

Page one of the prophetic message is the context of the Church, the society in which it has taken root. A study of it can yield much information about potential — potential responsiveness, high potential methods, potential fruit.

Page two is the institution of the Church itself. Here the data gets much more concrete, the prophetic message much more specific. For this message uncovers in actual fact what is being accomplished. It reveals God the Holy Spirit at work through his people. It illumines and clarifies the contextual data. It illustrates and modifies the conclusions drawn from a study of the context. It provides much specific information about what works best and how much fruit is possible. It makes possible a much clearer projection of what the Lord has in mind to be accomplished in the days ahead. It is a second point of reference making possible an accurate reading of the sextant.

From it optimum goals — neither too low nor too high — can be set, visions can be seen, dreams can be dreamed.

Again it can be asked if the Church does not already know what it is doing and therefore what it ought to be doing. The answer is usually "yes" in the specific, "no" in the general. Each local church, denominational headquarters, mission and parachurch organization knows more or less what is happening in its immediate sphere of influence.

It knows its methodologies, its organizational policies and practices, its approximate size and maybe — just maybe — its rate of growth.

But such information is quite sterile until seen in perspective of the remainder of the body of Christ in a nation. Until its policies, programs, methodologies, growth rates, fund-raising abilities, training programs, goals and many more specifics are compared with those of others, an accurate appraisal of effectiveness is all but impossible.

Inside the institution

By way of illustration, I again refer to the Church of Guatemala.

Steve Grant, then a missionary with Overseas Crusades but now with Dawn Ministries, spent several months on location in 1982. He gathered statistical data from all but a handful of denominations and parachurch organizations. He also interviewed two or three dozen leaders of these groups who spoke of the methodologies and reasons for growth or nongrowth in their ministries. From this, a well-focused picture began to emerge.

In the first place, we found a recurrent theme in the interviews. Almost all leaders said that the kind of people they were working with — be they students, children, women, rich, poor, city dweller, villager, Ladino or tribal — seemed to be quite responsive to the gospel. Almost everyone had seen the harvest potential in his or her own field, but few were seeing the whole picture. One result of our research was to put all these pieces together so that the whole could be seen.

The research uncovered a great number of sparkling stories and illustrations of excellent growth. Such stories are usually buried in denominational or regional pockets. But when they are discovered and communicated, they become great motivators for others.

One such story emerged from the little town of Chemelco. Believers in the tiny Nazarene church there decided that each one would personally bring others to Christ. In a short time, the handful grew to about 60. By the time they completed their first building, it was already full. So they built a larger one, only to find it also was full by the time it was completed. This circumstance was repeated *five times*. When Steve Grant interviewed Nazarene leaders he found this congregation was now building a temple to hold 2,500!

To a great deal of this kind of anecdotal material was added the hard facts of growth in Guatemala. Data compiled for the whole Church indicated that the overall rate of growth for the previous decade was an average of 12.5 percent a year. One significance of this is that each denomination could compare its growth with the average. The several denominations that were growing below this rate were challenged to believe they could do better. Those growing faster than the average were encouraged and many times came to believe they could do even better if they tried.

Another significance was the 12.5 percent AAGR (average annual growth rate) itself. Except to the very few with expertise in this area, this growth rate was almost meaningless until comparisons were made. One comparison was with the Church of other nations. When it was pointed out that this was one of the highest rates of growth for the Church of a whole country in the world, it was another great encouragement to evangelical leaders.

When data gathered from the denominations was further analyzed, many other significant points were to be made.

For example, when growth rates for the previous ten years were broken down into two five-year periods, it was found that many groups were getting significantly higher rates of growth in the second period. This indicated at least the possibility of the harvest becoming greater all the time.

It was also discovered that after many decades of the Pentecostal denominations growing much more rapidly than the non-Pentecostals, this trend was beginning to change. In fact, in the second five-year period it was found that eight major Pentecostal denominations were growing at a 14.7 percent AAGR, but a similar group of non-Pentecostals was growing at an 18.7 percent rate!

The significance of this was enormous. Older, sometimes larger denominations whose growth had definitely tailed off were coming back to vigorous new life, something that rarely happens.

Another significant trend was the number of rapidly growing churches springing up among the middle and even upper classes. A proliferation of church services held in first-class hotels that drew many hundreds was one indication of this breakthrough. This shattered a pattern that had existed in Latin America since the beginning of evangelical work there.

Other exciting phenomena included a rash of rapidly growing denominations that had been established by Guatemalans (rather than foreign mission societies) and the pockets of spectacular growth in various tribal groups.

In addition to these *facts* of growth, a study of *factors* of growth was made as well. Here are some of the factors that were looked at: goals, programs and methods for evangelism and church planting, training programs for lay workers on up through denominational leaders, financial policies and programs and their relationship to growth, organizational structures and their relationship to growth and a number of other items. When these were compiled and analyzed, it became even clearer why and how some were growing more rapidly than others. With this information, denominations could see not only that they *could* grow more rapidly, but *how* they could bring about this more rapid growth as well.

Church leaders in Guatemala were at least vaguely aware of some of this data, while some of the information was completely new. But it was not until it was systematically put together and interpreted that the incredible extent of the opportunity before them really struck home.

The Initial Rally and DAWN congress

This information was presented to the first group of about 75 leaders in 1983 in what we in Dawn Ministries now call the "Initial Rally." Using this data, we shared the observation that evangelicals could become 50 percent of the total population of the country by 1990 by increasing their overall AAGR to 17 percent. The response was overwhelming. There was almost immediate recognition that this was God's will for them.

(Later it would be found that some of the basic data was not up to date and that the 17 percent AAGR goal was a bit ambitious. At the same time, the basic prophetic message that the Church could become 50 percent of the population by 1990 was on target, as we shall see.)

The results of all this research and the prophetic message that emerged from it were put in a book entitled *La Hora de Dios Para Guatemala* (God's Hour for Guatemala), written jointly by Antonio Núñez, Galo Vasquez and myself.[1] This was published in time for the congress that followed.

When the Amanecer (Dawn) Congress with about 350 leaders was held a year after the Initial Rally there was virtually no questioning their ability and obligation to reach this goal. As a matter of fact, when various denominations sat down to make their own faith projections for the next five or six years, their goals were being set at around 30 percent instead of the suggested 17 percent AAGR.

The research and analysis of the context and the institution of the Church of Guatemala made possible the development of a prophetic message for the evangelicals of that country. Because the message was based on the reality of what God was doing in *their* particular situation, it spoke a powerful message to them. They concluded it truly was God's hour for Guatemala, and they set about their work with a new commitment and energy so that now "a whole new wave of evangelism and church planting is sweeping the country," according to one of their own top leaders.

Of course, in not every country will the possibilities for bringing people to Christ and into churches be as bright as in Guatemala. But the point is that when the Church of any country has a clear idea of the totality of what God is doing in their midst, they can much more realistically determine what the Lord would want to accomplish through them in the coming years. It can be anticipated that this usually will be much more than most dreamed possible.

This is the power of the prophetic message, the seventh ingredient in the DAWN package that makes it so dynamic.

Notes

1. Jim Montgomery, Emilio Antonio Núñez, Galo Vasquez, *La Hora de Dios Para Guatemala*, (Guatemala City: SEPAL, 1983). Also available in English through Dawn Ministries.

Chapter 11

Goals Release Tremendous Energy

The purest and simplest expression of the prophetic message in a DAWN project is the setting of national goals for the making of disciples and multiplication of local churches. Such goals distill the data of the researcher and the message of the Lord into a clear, understandable vision that can be easily communicated. The goals become the driving force that mobilizes God's people to efforts they never dreamed possible.

This is the next foundational aspect of a DAWN project:

8. GOALS RELEASE TREMENDOUS ENERGY.

Goal setting is the end result of the Nehemiah Effect. Once the children of Israel living in Jerusalem caught the vision of the restoration of the walls and the gates, they threw themselves into the task. The rabble that had been content to wallow in defeat and self-pity was now

143

energetically working together in a monumental task that had seemed way beyond its capabilities. Now they had a mental picture of the goal and rallied around its completion.

"For reasons I do not fully understand," writes Peter Wagner, "some power is released through setting positive goals that otherwise remains dormant. But although I cannot explain it as well as I wish I could, it is a biblical principle that God seems to honor.

"Goal setting is the modern equivalent to the biblical concept of faith, without which it is impossible to please God (Heb. 11:6). What is faith? 'Faith is the substance of things hoped for' (Heb. 11:1). Things hoped for are, of course, all future. Putting substance on the future is what happens in a faith projection (goal setting) exercise. . . ."[1]

Strong evidence that God honors the faith expressed in setting goals can be collected from all over the world. One illustration picked at random comes from the nation of Burundi in central Africa. A missionary with one denomination there said they had virtually stopped growing. From 1964 to 1974 they had increased only 28 percent, which amounts to an AAGR of only 2 percent.

But at a church growth workshop led by Vergil Gerber, they set a goal to grow ten times that fast in the next five years. This so galvanized the denomination into evangelism and church planting that in the next five years they actually grew at a rate almost *20 times* that of the previous decade!

Concerning this remarkable growth, Cho says, "The number one requirement for having real church growth — unlimited church growth — is to set goals."[2]

The C.M.A. model

From our experience in the Philippines, I observe that one of the dynamics of goal setting is that it forces the Church of a nation, a denomination or local church to focus all its energies on reaching that goal.

The Christian and Missionary Alliance there provides an example. They had grown from their first church in 1899 to 500 churches and about 25,000 members in 75 years. Then they set a goal to add 400 churches and 40,000 members in just *five* years.

To do this, they had to make many changes in their denomination. They set up new committees and training programs. They established hundreds of prayer cells. They set fund-raising goals and developed programs to reach them. They began publishing a monthly newspaper that kept all churches challenged and informed of their progress. They established a Census of Statistics and charged it with gathering, interpreting and reporting statistical data. They commissioned each local church to establish its own goals as well as committees for coordinating seminars, prayer groups and fund raising.

The cumulative effect of all this — and much more — was the development of a climate for growth in every facet of C.M.A. work in the Philippines. The normal resistance to change had been overcome. Pastors who at first laughed at the program became enthusiastic supporters. At the national level, seemingly insurmountable problems had been met and overcome.

A sleeping giant had been aroused and rallied to the cry of reaching more and more responsive Filipinos for the Savior.

Without their very challenging goals, these changes so essential for increased evangelism and church planting probably would never have been made. But with the goals and the changes the goals forced them to make, in just five years about 32,500 more people were brought to Christ and into local churches than would have been at their old rate of growth.

Furthermore, with the success of this program, they have continued to set new and ever more challenging goals. Currently they have a program called "Two, Two, Two." By this they mean they are aiming at two million members in 20,000 churches by the year 2000. Should they reach this goal, they will have exceeded what would have been expected by something like 1.9 million newly converted members in a 25-year period!

The Lord surely will not bless those who set goals for reasons of pride, competition or political benefit. But it does seem that goal setting is a biblical concept that does release tremendous energy and power for great advances in making disciples and planting churches.

Goals need careful consideration

Goal setting in a DAWN project actually takes place at several levels. At a DAWN Congress a national goal is suggested, wrestled with and ultimately agreed upon by the delegates.

Before the congress is over, leaders meet by denominational and parachurch groups and set preliminary goals for their organization. Many times, goals are then encouraged for each region of a denomination and even each local church.

Such goal setting can be a *dynamic ingredient* in the discipling of a nation.

It can be the expression of a clear and *forceful vision,* without which "the people perish" (Prov. 29:8).

It can be a powerful *expression of faith,* without which "it is impossible to please him" (Heb. 11:6).

If rightly discerned and established, a national goal can be the expression of a *prophetic message* to the people of God of a nation.

A national goal can provide the *unifying factor* for the body of Christ. It can help the body — in all its diversity and potential for division — begin to perceive itself as a body and to function as one.

Since we "are the body of Christ and individually members of it" (1 Cor. 12:27), we cannot expect to accomplish even a tiny part of our potential until we cooperate as the various parts of the body. A national goal helps make this possible without, at the same time, taking away the distinct value and function of each individual part.

Furthermore, a specific, numerical goal established for the discipling of a nation provides an effective and practical outlet for the feelings of concern for the people of one's native land. It puts teeth to the cry of a John Knox who proclaimed, "Give me Scotland or I die."

Indeed, the setting of a national goal is interlinked and inseparable from the 11 other foundational principles of a DAWN project. It can provide focus and direction for every ministry of every denomination, local church and para-church organization in the country.

At the same time, a national goal is not a cure-all nor a substitute for all the other spiritual and practical aspects of discipling a nation. If all the other ingredients are in place, the national goal can provide the catalyst to getting and keeping the program going. It is one crucial element, but only one.

An El Salvador case study

The way the Church in El Salvador went about setting its national goals provides an example of the process.

First, national Church leaders wanted to set goals that would have *historical perspective* and meaning. They decided, then, to set short-, medium- and long-range goals that their people could quickly identify with. The short-range goal would be for 1990, the end of the decade. The medium-range goal would be for 1996, the centennial year for the coming of protestant missionaries to El Salvador. The long-range goal would be for the year 2000, the end of the century and the end of the second millennium since the birth of Christ.

Second, the goals would have to be reasonable and *reachable.* Too high a goal would be discouraging and defeat the very purpose of goal setting. A goal that was too low, however, would not fire the enthusiasm and imagination necessary to speed the process of bringing men and women to Christ.

Third, the goals were to be set in terms of the relative *responsiveness* of the people. The forces of economy, politics, regional warfare and unrest and decline of the Roman Catholic Church in the country seemed to make people from all walks of life and backgrounds open to the gospel. The event that greatly increased this responsiveness and was used to awaken the Church to its tremendous opportunity was the massive earthquake of 1986. The goals would have to be set in light of the harvest that was quite evidently there.

Fourth, goals would have to be set in light of the *uncompleted task.* In El Salvador, about 20 percent of the population could be considered evangelical. That is high by many standards, but it still left *80 percent* of the population outside the fold. Much land had been conquered, but there remained "yet very much land to be possessed" (Josh. 13:1).

Fifth, leaders were encouraged to set goals in light of *past experience,* both inside El Salvador and in other countries of similar circumstances. In light of this, data gathered from all denominations of the country proved most helpful.

There were many ways to look at such data. This is where goal setting becomes an art and a deeply spiritual experience.

For one thing, Salvadoran Church leaders quickly found what others had learned: data never seems to be complete nor even necessarily accurate. One must dig and dig into the available information to come up with a meaningful pattern.

Even with the somewhat spotty information that researcher Bernardo Salcedo, a missionary with Dawn Ministries, was able to gather, it could be stated with some degree of confidence that the Church of the whole nation had grown at a very good AAGR of 11 percent for the previous five years.

With even greater difficulty it was determined that the AAGR had gone down to 7.7 percent for the last three years. Furthermore, some of the biggest denominations that made up the bulk of the Church were down to AAGR's of 5, 6 and 7 percent.

The overall picture, then, was one of a Church that had experienced great years of growth but now was in a period of decline. This would have to be a consideration in setting the national goals. At the same time, there were some denominations that were still growing at excellent to astounding rates of 15, 20 and 25 percent AAGR. In addition, many new denominations were springing up all the time and getting very good early growth. This tended to indicate that there was still much grain ready for harvest.

Leaders also took a look at the experience of the Philippines and Guatemala, countries and Churches of similar circumstance. It was seen that whereas the Philippine Church had been able to sustain an AAGR of about 10 percent over a period of twelve years, the Guatemalan Church had not yet achieved the 17 percent AAGR they had projected.

This data was bringing them closer to what might be a stretching yet attainable goal or goals for the nation. There was one further ingredient.

In the *sixth* place, they needed to set goals that were *clear and uncomplicated.* They would have to be easily communicated and easily remembered if the DAWN movement were going to catch fire and greatly speed the completion of the Great Commission in El Salvador.

This took a great deal more study and looking at the data from various angles. A chart of growth projections for new churches, for total memberships and for evangelical community each at growth rates of nine, ten, 11, 12, 13 and 14 percent AAGR's was developed. This took a considerable amount of calculating and making columns of numbers.

These then were pored over to find a set of goals that not only had historical meaning, were reasonable, took responsiveness into account, were set in light of the uncompleted task and were based on actual growth records, but also were clear and simple.

50 percent by 1996

As the leaders struggled through these issues, goals finally emerged that seemed to fit *all* the criteria. For it was discovered that at a 12 percent AAGR — a rate both challenging and achievable — the evangelical community of El Salvador would be 29.5 percent of the population by 1990, 50.5 percent by 1996 and 74 percent by AD 2000.

Without doing any injustice to accuracy, these were rounded off to 30 percent by 1990, 50 percent by 1996 (half the population by their centennial year!) and 75 percent by the end of the century.

To meet these goals for membership and evangelical community, they also set goals for the number of churches to be planted. This would require the same 12 percent AAGR and would provide the best method for reaching the goals for percent of population.

When the Executive Committee of the DAWN project — called Despertar (Awakening) '87 — heard this explanation, they immediately recognized this was what the Lord was calling them to reach for.

When the same full explanation and the goals themselves were presented to the Despertar Congress late in 1987, there was instant approval expressed through laughter and applause. They had come to the congress because of a great sense of urgency in reaching their troubled nation for Christ. There was a feeling of unity never before experienced to this extent according to their leaders. Many joyfully expressed a feeling of pending revival in the air.

Now the Church had a set of goals they believed was from the Lord. They now knew clearly what had to be done and they were committing themselves to do whatever was necessary to reach their new goals. They had expressed their faith in what the Lord would have them do, and a great sense of joy and exuberance was felt.

Once again, great energy had been released in the process of finding and setting goals for the discipling of their nation. This eighth powerful ingredient of the DAWN process, added to the other 11, was helping open the door to a greatly increased effort in the discipling of this Central American country.

Notes

1. C. Peter Wagner, "Why Body Evangelism Really Works," *Global Church Growth*, May/June 1983, p. 271.
2. Cho's whole remarkable story and rationale for goal setting can be found in his book *The Fourth Dimension* (Plainfield, N.J.: Logos International, 1979).

Chapter 12

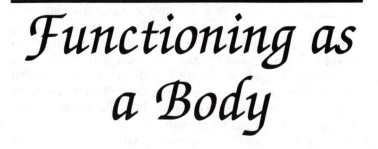

Functioning as a Body

We have seen in the past few decades a return to the biblical teaching on the body of Christ and the need for believers to function as a body. We have read the books on body life, heard the many cries for unity, attended inter-denominational and international conferences and congresses, organized a host of new structures that represent the whole body and cooperated in regional and nationwide evangelistic efforts.

This undoubtedly has been a healthy reemphasis on the unity we have in Christ. For when the body truly functions as a body, incredible power is unleashed. No truly dynamic strategy for the discipling of nations or completion of the Great Commission can be developed apart from this reality.

That is another reason why DAWN is such a powerful strategy. For, along with the other synergistic factors:

9. DAWN HELPS THE BODY OF CHRIST FUNCTION *AS* A BODY.

DAWN brings the body of Christ together in a way that takes advantage of the strengths of unity but avoids many of the pitfalls. For the unity comes in working towards a common goal rather than around specific projects.

Speaking to this point after the Dawn Congress in Guatemala in May 1984, Virgilio Zapata, the country's leading church historian, said, "[This congress] is very unique in the history of our Church. While denominations are challenged to work toward a common goal, in this case a 50 percent evangelical nation by 1990, they are not required to compromise their own individuality. We are free to be ourselves, to march under our own flags. But the key is that we go from here marching together."[1]

Working toward a common goal does not call for organizational unity and all the problems associated with that. The unity is expressed as each part of the body functions according to its own sense of calling and in line with its own policies and traditions concerning finance, organization, methods, historical background, and theological emphases towards a common, measurable goal.

Every part of the body — local churches, denominations, parachurch organizations, missions — helps and reinforces every other part as each plays its role in seeing churches multiplied. There is great strength in the whole body because it is working smoothly together in a common purpose and goal — the filling of the land with evangelical congregations.

Furthermore, with the Church of a nation now united around a long-range goal and strategy, such efforts as cooperative evangelistic campaigns smoothly fit in with that which is already in progress. The massive, public proclamation of the gospel greatly enhances the existing programs of evangelism and church planting rather than intruding on the activities of local churches and denominations.

For the body, now unified on a common goal that leads most directly to the discipling of its nation, can now so modify and fit each endeavor that it directly contributes to the accomplishing of the goal of church multiplication.

This leads to the next powerful ingredient of DAWN.

10. DAWN TAKES ADVANTAGE OF THE GREAT POTENTIAL OF DENOMINATIONS.

While the need for the body of Christ in a country to perceive itself as a body and to function as a body is acute, it is also true that the body is made up of many parts. For a body to function well, the parts must work in coordination.

For this to happen, however, each part of the body must be expected to do only that which it does best. As the Apostle Paul pointed out, "If the whole body were an eye, where would be the hearing?" (1 Cor 12:17).

In this analogy, each denomination and parachurch organization is a separate part of the body of Christ in a nation. When each is doing what it knows best how to do — but all towards the multiplication of churches — the body is functioning at its peak efficiency towards the completion of the Great Commission.

It seems to me that in the aftermath of World War II a great number of parachurch organizations sprang up because the Church was failing to fulfill its evangelistic mandate, among other things. But in all too many cases, instead of working "alongside" the Church and helping the Church do its task, these organizations did the work in place of the Church.

The DAWN strategy, however, encourages a balancing of Church and parachurch. It aims at restoring the Church to its primary ministry and function and, at the same time, encourages parachurch to aid and abet the Church, not replace it.

The crucial role of the local church

To a great extent, it is on the local level that the battle is won or lost. Local churches are a most crucial part of the body in world evangelization. Unless local churches equip and send out their people to do evangelism and church planting, a nation will not be filled with churches; it will not be discipled. Local churches must not only evangelize

155

and start daughter congregations in their own area and among their own kind of people — i.e., in their "Jerusalem" — but they must challenge and send out laborers to reach their own kind of people in more distant places. They must keep "all Judea" in mind.

Local churches need to prepare their people for reaching slightly different kinds of people near by and more distant. They must reach their "Samaria."

It is also primarily at the local level that Christians will get a vision and calling for the "uttermost parts of the earth": totally different kinds of people both close at hand and in distant lands.

When evangelists or missionaries are thus sent from the local church to engage in M1 (missions 1, etc.), M2, or M3, they go out to plant local churches and train others to do the same.

The slogan "The Local Church Can Change the World" has a solid basis in truth. Local churches are the front-line trenches where the spiritual warfare of "conquering" a nation for Christ gets done.

There is still the reality, however, that *one* local church cannot do it alone. It takes the combined efforts of thousands of local churches to disciple a nation, and millions of local churches to "change the world."

This multitude of local churches must be broken down into manageable segments where they can be motivated, trained and mobilized for the task. Denominations represent those "manageable segments." They are the structures already in place that have the ability to mobilize groups of congregations for church multiplication.

"The only built-in system"

In this respect, DAWN helps resurrect the great potential of denominations for the discipling of nations and for world evangelization. When I was speaking on this point in his MC522 class at Fuller Seminary in April 1987, Peter Wagner amplified on the subject by saying:

We may or may not like it, but in most nations of the world, most Christian work is carried on within denominational structures. As a matter of fact, the only uniform, worldwide, built-in system of delivering programs to the grass roots is denominations. Many parachurch leaders don't realize that.

One of the chief mystiques about DAWN is that it recognizes the denominational structures. It celebrates the denominational structures. It does not ask any denomination to compromise. And furthermore, it does not explicitly try to dilute denominational competition.

We may say "we shouldn't have competition." But in the places in the world where the gospel has spread the fastest, there is competition. Now we want that competition to be a Christian type of competition.

What each denomination does is up to it. DAWN is not telling it what to do. It does not compromise the aggressiveness or the competition of the denominations.

The point of unity focuses on the harvest. That is a lot different from the ecumenical movement where the point of unity is generally focused on the "barns" that are supposed to contain the harvest.

If we focus the unity on the harvest, we can accomplish much more than we can otherwise.

Denominational programs in the Philippines

Interviews with a number of denominational leaders at Congress '85 in the Philippines highlighted this aspect of the great potential of denominations. One after another of

157

them said something to the effect that were it not for the DAWN-type seminars and congresses held in 1974 and 1980 they would simply have continued using their old methodologies and growing at their old, slower rates.

A summary of some of the denominational programs will help make the point.

The C.M.A. work mentioned in the last chapter provided a good model, but there are many others. The Conservative Baptists, for example, came to the Philippines much later than the C.M.A., but they have been pace setters in recent years. When they launched their "Operation 200" program in 1972, they had only 31 churches and 1,657 members. By faith they set a goal of 200 churches and 10,000 members by 1981.

On reaching that goal — which required the very high AAGR of 20 percent — they set their sights on the next five years in which time they set and reached the goal of doubling their membership to 20,000.

Their new target is 60,000 members by 1990, a program that requires an average annual growth of 25 percent! This current program, while quite visionary, is based on 13 years of solid experience in carrying out denomination-wide growth projects. So their growth goal that might seem impossible to others, seems to them very bold and challenging on the one hand, but within their capability with the Lord's help on the other.

In 1972 the Southern Baptists began their drive to grow from 180 congregations to 3,000 within a decade. Though they did not reach this goal — in part because it was unrealistic in the first place — they did grow much more rapidly during that period than they had in the previous decade.

Despite their unreachable goal, the Southern Baptists were not daunted, at least in Mindanao where a majority of their work exists. Following that first experience, this district developed a project called "Strategy 1085 by 1985." This called for an increase from 447 churches to 1,085 in just five years.

During the period of this program they grew at a very excellent rate of 16 percent a year, well above the national average in the Philippines, and, incidentally, about ten times as fast as their parent denomination in the U.S. They fell short of their goal, but were still greatly exceeding their prior growth. Now their third program is under way and is called "20,000 Disciples in 2,000 Churches," a goal they have targeted for 1990.

One of the fastest rates of growth in the country has been achieved by the Association of Baptist Churches of the Philippines (ABCOP) denomination. They grew from 1,252 members in 1974 to 8,454 in 1981, an AAGR of 31 percent! At about that time they launched "Expansion 100" which expressed their goal of adding 100 churches to the 106 that existed in 1981. They also fell short of this goal set for 1985. But as so often happens, they were so thrilled with the good results they did achieve that they set a new program called "1,000 by 2,000," that is, 1,000 churches by the end of the century.

Historic results

In all, at least 15 denominations in the Philippines developed such programs, some of them now in the second, third or fourth generation. The existence of these far-sighted programs — and many others in Guatemala and a growing number of other nations — herald one of the most remarkable movements in at least the recent history of the Church worldwide. Never before have so many denominations in one country developed so many intentional programs of growth and achieved such remarkable results.[2]

For the Church as a whole, extensive research indicates that overall growth has been at least twice as fast each year in the past 14 years as it had been in each year of the previous ten. Now, with at least 21,000 evangelical churches in existence, the Church of the Philippines is on target for growing from about 5,000 congregations in 1974 to 50,000, and perhaps many more, by AD 2000.

This remarkable growth has come about through awakening the great potential of denominations. When a whole denomination sets a major goal, it has tremendous ability to focus all its resources on reaching that goal. It has the built-in authority structure to make something happen. It has the natural *esprit de corps* necessary to mobilize its financial and personnel resources. It has the muscle to get something significant done.

The DAWN approach encourages denominations to develop and use their muscle for the discipling of nations through such programs of church multiplication. It challenges denominations to carry out research that will show them where and how fast churches can be planted. It motivates them to set challenging yet realistic goals and to devise plans and allocate resources in sufficient strength to reach those goals. It encourages them to abandon methods and programs that inhibit church multiplication and devise methods of church planting that are continuously reproducible on a local level.

DAWN suggests to denominations the need for refocusing their Bible and theological school curricula for training church planters and for mobilizing and training their laypeople for this endeavor. It helps them focus radio, evangelistic, and various institutional work on the prime task of church planting. It opens their eyes to the need for sending missionaries to unreached or slightly reached people groups and homogeneous units within their country.

DAWN helps catalyze the tremendous potential within denominational structures for a direct assault on the discipling of whole nations. But it also encourages a strong role for parachurch organizations as we see in the next ingredient:

11. DAWN HELPS PARACHURCH ORGANIZATIONS TRULY FUNCTION "ALONGSIDE" THE CHURCH IN THE DISCIPLING OF NATIONS.

At the other end of the spectrum from the denomination

is the parachurch organization. The DAWN challenge to these groups is to a diligent reexamination of ministries and a restructuring of them so as to provide maximum help to denominations and local churches in church multiplication. The same can be said for mission societies.

A seminary church-planting program

The Evangelical Theological Seminary of Indonesia (ETSI) is an example of one such ministry. It is a parachurch organization in that it is a school, it is not connected with any particular denomination and it has as a guiding principle the idea of helping local churches and denominations.

ETSI could have become like the majority of other Bible and theological schools throughout the world in turning out students who knew sound doctrine and how to study and teach the Word, but knew little or nothing about evangelism and church planting.

But Chris Marantika, its Indonesian founder, had another vision. He wanted to be truly parachurch. He wanted to work "alongside" the Church, helping it accomplish its primary task. He wanted to work most directly at discipling the whole nation of Indonesia by filling it with evangelical congregations.

So he said to local church and denomination leaders that he would not only train their young people in the Word, but would also train them in evangelism and church planting. Furthermore, they would actually plant a church as a requirement for graduation, and the church would become part of the denomination involved.

Marantika opened his tiny school with a big vision in the Fall of 1979 with 15 students. By the end of 1987 there were 208 students who had already seen 19,526 decisions for salvation, 9,340 baptisms and 438 house churches planted! Based on experience so far, Marantika estimates 90 percent of all students will actually plant a church during their four years at the school.

Marantika's "One, One, One" vision

Now Marantika has a vision and plan for his "One, One, One" program mentioned earlier. He is planning to begin an increasing number of two-year training centers each year until there are 415 scattered throughout the nation by AD 2015. Through the church-planting efforts of these students he expects to turn over enough new churches to cooperating denominations so that there will be one in every village of the country at the end of this one generation, that is, by the year 2015. Furthermore, Marantika has now begun planning for a major conference that will aim at motivating whole denominations for the setting of church-planting goals towards the national goal of "One, One, One."

Not all Bible schools are blessed with the vision, ability and energy of a Chris Marantika, nor are they all located in areas as responsive to the gospel. But certainly most Bible schools of the world could be reoriented towards producing workers with a vision and ability to multiply churches.

And this is just one type of parachurch ministry. Everything else from door-to-door literature distribution, to radio and TV broadcasting, to film showing, to translation, to city-wide crusades, to cross-cultural outreach, to a host of other activities could be redesigned to make church planting at least one major, direct outcome of the ministry.

By helping the whole body of Christ of a nation focus on a national church-planting goal, DAWN helps parachurch groups clarify their roles and modify their plans to work synergistically alongside the Church in the discipling of a nation.

As the whole body of Christ in nations around the world and in the whole world begins more and more to perceive itself as a body and begins to function more as a body, the task of planting 7 million more congregations will be greatly enhanced.

Notes

1. Ted Olsen, "Amanecer '84 Ushers in New Life from Ancient Ruins," *Global Church Growth*, May/June 1984, p. 374.
2. The denominational projects in the Philippines have been analyzed and compared with others around the world. Several common denominators were found among them and put into the article "13 Steps to a Successful Growth Program." This can be found in Appendix I.

Chapter 13

A Strategy for 7 Million Churches

We come now to the twelfth and last foundational principle that seems to make DAWN so powerful and so attractive to many. When we put all the first 11 ingredients together into one package, we find that:

12. DAWN PROVIDES A FRAME OF REFERENCE FOR A NATIONAL STRATEGY.

On the morning I began writing this chapter, I picked up a pamphlet sent by the Assemblies of God concerning their "Decade of Harvest" project. In it they quote a certain Clausewitz whom they identify as a great Prussian military strategist:

> The best strategy is always to be very strong at the decisive point. . . . There is no more imperative and no simpler law for strategy than to keep

the forces concentrated. No portion is to be separated from the main body unless called away by some urgent necessity. . . . All forces which are available and destined for a strategic object should be simultaneously applied to it . . . [and] compressed into one act and one movement.

Where was Clausewitz when I needed him in 1968? I had just become field director for O.C. in the Philippines and was trying to develop a strategy for the discipling of that nation.

I could see that our team had many good ministries, but felt they did not add up to anything in particular. I wanted to bring them together into a coherent strategy. If I could have explained this with the silver tongue of a Clausewitz, perhaps some of my missionaries would not have gone home or transferred to Singapore. I might even have gotten along better with the home office.

A laundry list of ministries

Instead, I just looked at our laundry list of ministries in bewilderment.

We had massive conferences for thousands of pastors. We helped bring the Billy Graham team and held other evangelistic activities. We were pioneers in sports evangelism, gaining the attention of the whole country by playing their national basketball teams. There was a film ministry with about 65 titles for churches to rent. We published *Crusader* Magazine for 5,000 pastors and workers. We had the Norm Nelson radio ministry that was perhaps the most popular program in evangelical circles in the country. Best of all, we handled the Bible Investigation School, a correspondence course that enrolled tens of thousands of Filipinos.

When I joined the team I added a national Christian education ministry that within a few years held over 50 regional Sunday school conventions, a research function that in cooperation with others produced several books, and even a Young Life ministry.

These were just the major ministries. We had many others as well.

What we didn't have was a strategy. Each of these excellent activities for which we became well known and highly respected was an arrow thrust out in its own direction. There was no target or focal point. The "forces" were not "concentrated" nor were they "destined for a strategic object" and "compressed into one act and one movement."

There was no basis for deciding priorities. Ministry was left to the whim and interests of various missionaries. We simply hoped that somehow all these activities would result in the Church of the Philippines being equipped and mobilized for the discipling of its nation.

Concentrating the forces

The truth is, I didn't very well articulate what I was trying to do. I didn't exactly know. But I brashly plunged ahead, getting into more and more trouble as I went. For how could one question the validity of the Bible correspondence course with its thousands of students? Or sponsoring the weekly prayer meeting for all of Manila's missionaries? (One of my worst mistakes was dropping this!) Or any of the other crucial activities developed by such gifted missionaries?

Little by little, however, I began trying to concentrate the forces at the decisive point. By now I had presented my paper at the All Philippines Congress on Evangelism that suggested the goal of 10,000 Lay, Evangelistic Group Studies (LEGS) in the country. That would be the target we would try to thrust all our arrows at.

Instead of generalized pastors' conferences, for instance, we began putting more money and personnel into seminars on LEGS.

Concerning the Bible correspondence course, we discovered there were 21 separate items that had to be printed, stored, handled and mailed in order to complete the four lessons. These were modified and published in one booklet that churches could now buy and use with their LEGS groups. With this change, the Bible course was now contributing directly to the goal of 10,000 evangelistic Bible study groups. Furthermore, the *churches* were now using this tool instead of us doing the work for them. On top of that, with this stroke alone we freed a major part of our budget for other ministries that would contribute more directly towards the goal of 10,000 LEGS.

I next wrote Bud Schaeffer that we didn't want the Venture for Victory basketball team he was planning to send. Our feeling was that such a rivalry had developed between VV and Philippine national team that the ministry effectiveness was reduced almost to zero. I did ask Schaeffer, however, if he could provide ten players who could come for a year. They could play in hundreds of barrios that would go crazy over an American team. The players could give testimonies at half-time and invite people to enroll in LEGS groups sponsored by local churches. (He did, and several hundred LEGS were started.)

We dropped *Crusader* Magazine and sponsored a new publication called *Acts 29*. In this periodical we dropped all the general features concerning family and ministry and saw to it that the main thrust related to the goal of 10,000 LEGS. *Crusader* was not bad. In fact, it had been one of my main personal ministries. And there was a need for it. But when we replaced it with *Acts 29*, not only did our ministry become more pointed and strategic but another organization better equipped for such a publishing venture as *Crusader* started a magazine that became *the* voice for evangelicals in the country.

It might have been expected we would drop city-wide evangelistic crusades in favor of the more personalized evangelism of the home Bible study groups. In fact, we increased them, holding 21 in my last 18 months in the Philippines. But they were crusades with a difference.

They were so organized that LEGS groups provided both a source for the unsaved who would attend and the follow-up strategy for those who would come forward.

Some ministries we spun off to national staff members. Betty Javalera, for example, got some help from C.N.E.C. (Partners International) and turned our Christian education ministry into one of the finest in Asia. (It is called PACE, an acronym for Philippine Association for Christian Education.) Eli Yasi persisted through many hard years to make the Young Life ministry a very potent one. We in effect gave our 65 Christian films to another organization that was already in this ministry.

Other ministries were modified or dropped so that now all — or at least most — of our energies and resources were focused on reaching this one goal. To the glory of God, the goal was reached and exceeded. And from that experience came the goal of 50,000 churches by AD 2000 and ultimately the DAWN movement now spreading throughout the world.

DAWN summarized

That was my experience in modifying, dropping and adding ministries so that a strategy "very strong at the decisive point" for the discipling of the Philippines was developed.

I have given credit to Clausewitz for suggesting we need strategy, but there is no doubt in my mind that a strong rationale could be developed from scripture as well. Consider the parable of the talents, for example (Mt. 25:15ff). The three servants were to be held accountable for how they invested the resources entrusted to them. Are we not likewise to give an account of how we handled the resources entrusted to us as they relate to completing the final command of this same Lord? That really is what strategy is all about.

Our point here is that developing a DAWN project in a

country has the potential of seeing our resources used to best advantage. DAWN can result in an effective national strategy being developed. Adopting a specific national goal — as well as denominational, parachurch and local church goals — opens the door for existing ministries to be so modified or dropped and new ministries added that a powerful strategy emerges. In a DAWN project, this process can be carried out in local churches, in denominations, in parachurch organizations and at the national level.

This is what DAWN is all about. It is an attempt under the guidance of the Holy Spirit to mobilize the whole body of Christ in a whole nation in a strategy for the discipling of that nation. As this spreads to all nations, it becomes a strategy for world evangelization, for completing the Great Commission.

It is a strategy that:

1. is Christ-centered in its emphasis on seeing him made incarnate in every cluster of 500 to 1,000 people in the world;

2. is built on the comprehensive plan of God who is not willing that any should perish;

3. focuses on the systematic occupation of the land;

4. takes advantage of the practical and emotional values of a whole-country approach;

5. releases the incredible power of information;

6. delivers a prophetic message to the Church;

7. harnesses the vast energies inherent in working towards a measurable, time-bound goal;

8. emphasizes the "best method under heaven;"

9. helps the body of Christ function effectively as a body;

10. releases the great potential of denominations;

11. encourages parachurch organizations to function truly "alongside" the Church;

12. provides a frame of reference for national and worldwide strategy for the discipling of the nations.

Each of these 12 ingredients of DAWN is powerful in itself. When they are put together in symbiotic relationship, their potential is enormous.

They provide a strategy that, under the hand of God, can help us work most directly towards completing the Great Commission by planting 7 million additional churches by AD 2000.

Part Three

How DAWN Works

Chapter 14

Beginning a DAWN Project

As we tried to demonstrate in the last chapter, DAWN is designed to be a long-range strategy that will result in hastening the completion of the Great Commission in a country and in all countries.

The desired outcome of a DAWN project is a revitalized evangelistic and church-planting life style that becomes a habitual part of local churches, denominations, missions and other parachurch organizations. It provides a long-range strategic framework into which a great variety of local, regional and national events can be fitted. It helps the body of Christ in a nation perceive itself as a body and to function as a body in a most direct way towards the discipling of that nation.

A DAWN project is not an event but a cyclical process. Each cycle consists of several steps or events. When the first series of events is completed, the process begins anew. This can continue for ten, 20 or 30 years, so long as it is viable or until the Lord himself returns.

So far in this book we have given the background, principles and some models of DAWN projects. Now it is time to give in chronological order at least the basic steps and events of a DAWN project. To give detailed instruc-

tions on how to carry out DAWN would take another complete book or set of training manuals. These are in process.
What follows in this chapter and the next is a brief
summary statement concerning the chronology of a DAWN
project.

1. RESPOND TO THE MESSAGE OF DAWN MINISTRIES.

The obvious first step is for the vision and concepts of
DAWN to be communicated to the right people. This is the
primary task of the little mission agency we call Dawn
Ministries. Our role is not to sponsor DAWN projects but to
serve others in implementing this strategy.

To do this we have at present four missionaries that
have been mentioned in several places in this book. All of
us speak English, while Wolfgang Fernandez and Bernardo
Salcedo also speak Spanish and Steve Grant speaks French.
We are in contact with several others with background and
experience in DAWN that we trust will join us in the future.
Our ultimate goal is a team of 12 missionaries. With these
and an office staff of eight to ten, we feel we can see
DAWN spread to every country in the world before the end
of the century.

This staff carries out several ministries designed to fan
the flames of the DAWN movement and equip leaders for
individual projects. We publish books, periodicals, papers,
national case studies (the prophetic message for a country),
manuals and other materials. These report on DAWN
projects, explain what DAWN is and how it works and give
further instruction on how to put on a DAWN project.[1]

This staff is also available on a personal basis to John
Knoxers and others interested in DAWN. Each of our men
take three or four international trips a year for seminars,
training, research and personal consultations. We also
carry out extensive correspondence with John Knoxers and
others.

When possible, Dawn Ministries brings John Knoxers

together for some dynamic fellowship and interaction. About 40 of us gathered at our first John Knox Fellowship in London in November 1987. We also had sessions with our 'Knoxers at the Singapore AD 2000 Consultation and Lausanne II in Manila, both in 1989. Other gatherings of the whole group or parts of it are planned.

For the world Christian who supports and prays for world evangelization, I should mention that we are a faith mission. We estimate in the next eight years it will take about $7 million for the personal support and ministries of our anticipated staff of 20. With this relatively small amount we expect to see DAWN established for every country of the world with the ultimate result that millions more will be swept into the Kingdom and the completion of the Great Commission hastened. We also want to raise a like amount as seed money for John Knoxers to get projects under way, in particular by getting the research done.

2. IDENTIFY THE "JOHN KNOXER."

Above all, the purpose of Dawn Ministries is to locate, train, equip, counsel, stand by and support in every way possible the key person in developing a DAWN project, that is, the John Knoxer.

In developing anything as massive and extensive as mobilizing the entire body of Christ of a nation for a direct assault on the discipling of that nation, somebody has to do a lot of work! That is the person we call the "John Knoxer," the person who says "Give me my country or I die."

The John Knoxer's task is at once awesome and delicate. Such a person must have a vision for and commitment to the discipling of his or her whole nation. This person must have or be able to gain the respect and cooperation of the whole body of Christ in all its diversity. He or she must have the organizational structure including the personnel and financial resources to make a sustained effort in mobilizing all the denominations, independent churches, missions and other parachurch organizations around a major, nationwide, long-term goal of evangelism and church planting.

To find such an organization with a John Knoxer at its head might sound an impossible task. In reality, it isn't. There are organizations in various nations that fit this role, or could fit with some modifications. In some cases new organizations could be developed for this purpose.

In the DAWN models that were developed in the Philippines and Guatemala, for example, field teams of Overseas Crusades played this role. To a considerable extent, they were able to function as true servants of the Church on the one hand while taking effective leadership in mobilizing the whole body of Christ on the other. Though never without struggle and hardship, they were able to supply enough trained leaders, office space and equipment, secretarial and "go-fer" help and a certain amount of money raised from abroad to keep some essential machinery in motion.

There are other countries where O.C. teams can and will function in this role. Ted Olsen, for example, has seen DAWN get under way in Zimbabwe. Greg Gripentrog, Asia Director for O.C., presently is encouraging all the teams under his jurisdiction to support current and emerging projects in the Philippines, Indonesia, India, Taiwan and Japan.

Other such structures are becoming involved. In talks with Loren Cunningham, I learned that there are at least two nations where Youth With A Mission teams have the vision, ability and resources for this role. If the idea caught on within YWAM, they could provide such a structure in many nations of the world.

The same could be said for Campus Crusade. DAWN projects in any number of countries could provide the vehicle for reaching their goal of helping denominations plant one million churches by AD 2000. Adonai Leiva, their field director in El Salvador, has already modeled this in the leadership he has taken in developing the DAWN project in his country.

Several organizations are already functioning in this capacity in Africa. Johan Engelbrecht, founder and director of the Institute for Church Growth In Africa, is well along in the DAWN process in South Africa and has seen the vision take hold in Namibia and Malawi as well. Evangelism Resources, under the leadership of Willys and Thelma Braun, has developed a DAWN-type project in Zaire, as has Ross Campbell of New Life for All in Ghana. Reuben Ezemadu, Secretary for the Nigeria Evangelical Missions Association and Director of Christian Missionary Foundation, has already plunged deep into the research phase of DAWN.

Rob Gill of the Japan Church Growth Institute has been gradually introducing the concept to Japanese leaders, and Bobby Gupta, President of the Hindustan Bible College, has seen a DAWN project launched by a large group of leaders in India. This list does not exhaust the organizations we are in contact with that could function in the capacity of a John Knox.

Based on our experience, it is our belief that John Knoxers exist in (or for) every land of the world. They have the burden and the ability. They are just waiting to be discovered, equipped and released for the discipling of a nation!

Functioning as a John Knoxer, of course, does not necessarily require any relationship to Dawn Ministries. DAWN-type projects in Canada and Taiwan, for example, were under way even before leaders there heard about DAWN. Such a circumstance, by the way, is another confirmation that the whole idea is truly of the Lord.

When a potential John Knoxer has been identified in a country by whatever process, however, the first major step towards a DAWN project has been taken.

3. COMPLETE THE INITIAL RESEARCH AND ANALYSIS.

By now it should be clear that data is the foundation

upon which the whole DAWN concept is built. Correct data of the right kind is that which produces the Nehemiah Effect. It overcomes inertia in the Church, it motivates the Church, it keeps the Church moving and on target.

So the first task of the John Knoxer and his or her organization is to do the research and develop a base of data. One or more workers trained in church growth research and analysis need from one to six months of library and field research on the context and institution of the Church in order to gather the facts. The amount of time necessary depends on the size of the country, the size of the Church and the amount of time workers can give to this activity.

Gaining credibility

The very process of gathering data gives authority to those who would attempt to mobilize the Church for a nationwide project. It is relatively easy to reject a potential leader because he or she is too young or too old, from the wrong denomination or country, from the wrong tribe or region or speaks the wrong dialect. But it is difficult for an honest believer who is concerned about the lost to fight against the facts. It quickly becomes evident that the researcher is gathering data that will be of great interest and use. The researcher is in the process of becoming a sought-after authority on the Church in that country.

The research phase also begins the process of communicating the vision of DAWN. While interviewing various leaders, questions are being asked of the researcher. To whom will this information be revealed? How will it be used? Answering these natural questions gives the researcher an opportunity to explain: The DAWN committee is interested to know more about how the Spirit of God is at work in their organization so that this can be an encouragement to others. They want to develop a picture of the whole body of Christ in the nation so the Church can work more effectively at discipling its nation. This picture of the Church will be put in a book that will be presented at a DAWN Congress where the Church will determine what the Spirit is saying to them for the future.

What data is needed?

We labeled step three "Complete *initial* research." The data necessary to overcome the inertia of the Church and get it rolling in a powerful nationwide project is only the beginning. After the first DAWN Congress is completed, there will be need for data to be compiled year after year. We will come back to this important topic, but for now make a few comments on the data required for this initial step.

How much data is needed at this point in the DAWN process?

Just enough so that a strong case can be presented to show how responsive the peoples of the country are to the gospel, to what extent the various peoples have been identified and discipled, how fast and how effectively the Church has been growing in its various branches, what basic methodologies seem to be producing the best growth and, most important, how fast should the Church be able to grow in the coming years.

The research should also produce a basic picture of the context, that is, all those forces of society at work outside the Church. The Guatemala model in chapter 10 describes the nature of this contextual data.

Completing such research may sound like a tall order and in truth it should not be underestimated. At the same time, it might not be as complicated as it sounds. Bob Waymire accomplished it in less than two months in the Philippines, and Steve Grant did it in three months — without being able to speak fluent Spanish — in Guatemala. Wolfgang Fernandez spent three months in New Zealand where he spent only one-third of his time on research.

The Church Growth Survey Handbook

The data that is required can be gathered essentially by following the steps in *The Church Growth Survey Handbook*.[2] The *Handbook* will also demonstrate how the data can be processed into charts and graphs and then analyzed.

It is first necessary to develop a complete list of every denomination, mission and parachurch organization in the country. Then, the head or a responsible leader of each group will be visited and interviewed. The interview will consist primarily in filling out the forms in the *Handbook*.

The most crucial data relates to the statistical record of each denomination. You will want to discover its number of active members, average attendance, number of churches and chapels, number of evangelistic Bible study groups, number of ordained pastors and in some cases other statistics. This data needs to be gathered for each year of the denomination's existence, or at least for the previous 11 years. The latter makes it possible to determine AAGR's for the past ten years.

Not by a long shot is all this information readily available. In many cases it will take repeated visits and perhaps some careful estimating as well as some spot visits to local churches to come up with fairly reliable information.

In addition to the concrete data, many other things will be learned in following the questions of the *Handbook*. Included will be some history of the denomination, a listing of growth projects and methodologies that are being used, some idea of the kinds of people that are being reached through the denomination, some insights into how responsive these kinds of people are and further insights into how the methodologies and practices of the denomination or group relate to their growth or nongrowth.

This kind of statistical data does not apply to most parachurch organizations and some missions, but much will be learned from them as well.

In order to gather all the right kinds of data and to effectively analyze it in most cases will require some training of researchers. This is an area where Dawn Ministries and others can many times be of help.

4. DEVELOP THE PROPHETIC MESSAGE.

From an analysis of the data indicating what the Holy Spirit is doing in and through society and the Church comes the message of what this suggests for the future. This is perhaps the most sensitive and crucial aspect of the whole process, for the Church will be motivated to bold new action only to the degree that it believes that the challenge is truly from the Lord. Jesus said that his sheep hear his voice and they will not follow another.

The researcher with his or her bank of information that has been carefully analyzed now becomes "the man of the hour." This person becomes like one of the tribe of Issachar. You remember how David numbered the men who were ready for battle (1 Chron. 12). There were 6,800 men of Judah, for example, who were spear carriers and ready for battle. The brave warriors of Ephraim numbered 20,800 and the experienced soldiers of Zebulun who were prepared for battle with every type of weapon numbered 50,000.

But for the tribe of Issachar, only their 200 chiefs were numbered. These were the men "who understood the times and knew what Israel should do" (12:32). They were a tiny band compared with the thousands from the other tribes, but they played a role all out of proportion to their size. For what good is a vast army that does not know how to utilize its forces for victory?

That is the value of the researcher. This person can so gather and analyze information about the context and the institution of the Church that he or she comes to an understanding of the times and therefore can point out to the Church what it should do. The Church cannot proceed effectively until it clearly perceives the direction the wind of the Spirit is blowing.

183

The prophetic message essentially communicates the vision of how fast the Church ought to be able to grow over the next five to ten years and what methodologies will be most productive in bringing about that growth. It is the message that provides the content for personal contacts, messages delivered in churches, seminars, congresses, articles, books and other communications.

To provide a thorough, logical and consistent message that can be studied and prayed over at length, this message is put in book form. It thereby becomes the basic document for the DAWN movement in a given country. It can be distributed to and studied by participants at the DAWN Congress and used by denominations and in seminars throughout the nation after that.

Insights from Guatemala

La Hora de Dios Para Guatemala (God's Hour for Guatemala) is a good sample of the kind of book that can be written and produced.[3] It was based on the research completed by Steve Grant during a three-month period in 1982. After this data was carefully analyzed, I wrote several chapters of the book that included the following:

"Spying Out the Land"
>(Introduction to the concept of research and preliminary findings concerning responsiveness)

"The Harvest is Plenteous"
>(Demonstrating the great responsiveness in Guatemala)

"The Facts of Growth"
>(Analysis of church growth statistics of denominations, regions, trends)

"The Factors of Growth"
>(What methodologies and models produced the best growth)

"Special Factors of Indigenous Growth"
>(Information about work in the large Indian population)

"Becoming 50 Percent Evangelical"
> (Explains how this goal was arrived at, what it means and how to achieve it)

"A Church for Every Guatemalan"
> (Demonstrates the basic methodology for reaching the 50 percent goal)

"Recommendations to the Church of Guatemala"
> (How to develop a DAWN project and reach their goals)

"A Pattern to Follow"
> (Brief description of the Philippine model)

Five other chapters were written by Latins who were involved in the Amanecer (Dawn) project. Emilio Antonio Núñez, the brilliant theologian and teacher, did the final editing of the whole book and also wrote two chapters:

"What Type of Churches?"
> (A biblical model of what newly planted churches ought to be like)

"Who Will Make Disciples?"
> (A call to all agencies that make up the body of Christ in Guatemala to commit themselves to the task)

Galo Vasquez, then serving as Executive Secretary of Conela and now President of Vela in Mexico, wrote three inspirational chapters:

"To Guatemala with Love"
"To All the Nation"
"From Guatemala with Love"

Writing and publishing the prophetic message

The writing and publishing of the "prophetic message" in book form can take from a month or two up to a year, depending on how it is approached. If there is one editor for such a book, some individual chapters, especially the inspirational ones, can be assigned to various church leaders. It is good, though not necessary, if the book can be written or at least edited by a qualified national.

In some countries, the prophetic message was put together in loose-leaf form in a large binder and distributed at the Congress itself. That took much less time and seemed to work just as well. The important matter is to get into written form the material that clearly shows what it is God the Holy Spirit is doing in a nation and the Church of a nation and through this demonstrate what it is God evidently wants to accomplish through the Church in the coming period of years.

These first four steps in a DAWN process all lead to the first public meeting related to a DAWN project. This will be explained in the next chapter which will also take us through the rest of the cycle of a DAWN project.

Notes

1. Appendix II gives a current list of these items and how they may be acquired. Our free, quarterly publication, *DAWN Report,* along with all its other features about DAWN, publishes an update on new materials as they are available.
2. Bob Waymire and Peter Wagner, *The Church Growth Survey Handbook,* (published by *Global Church Growth* Magazine, 1983), available from Overseas Crusades or Dawn Ministries.
3. The original Spanish version of this book is available from Dawn Ministries. An English version is also available in typescript form. A few of the purely inspirational chapters have been dropped from this edition.

Chapter 15

The DAWN Congress and Beyond

With the initial research completed and the prophetic message taking shape, the John Knoxer and his or her organization are now ready to spring into action in presenting the DAWN idea to the Church of the nation. The first four steps have been completed. Now it is time for the first public meeting.

5. HOLD AN INITIAL RALLY.

In the process of gathering data and interviewing various Church leaders, relationships are being developed and vision communicated for a united assault on the discipling of the nation.

There comes a time when some of these leaders become excited about and committed to the idea of a DAWN project. A small group of them can now be formed into an ad hoc committee that will help introduce DAWN to the rest of the Church of the nation. It will be their job to supervise the first public presentation of DAWN in what we call an Initial Rally.

The purpose of this rally is to present some of the initial findings of the research and to get goal ownership for a DAWN project. The John Knoxer and a few others can believe in the strategy, but unless the whole Church of a nation as represented by a group of its leaders gains ownership, it will be useless to proceed.

Since that is the case, much prayer should be offered and no effort spared in getting the right people to attend and ensuring a top-rate program for this Initial Rally. The "right" people are denomination, mission and parachurch heads that represent a broad spectrum of the Church at its highest level. Every evangelical tradition from Pentecostal to mainline to conservative denominations should be represented. There should also be representatives from major mission societies and parachurch organizations. These are the leaders that, should they decide to proceed with a DAWN project, will be able to mobilize the rest of the body of Christ in the country.

The program for the Initial Rally calls for the best speakers and music. But the greatest drawing card is the data that has been gathered. Busy leaders will come if they are convinced reliable information is available about the growth of the Church in their nation.

Such was the case in New Zealand in September of 1987. When an ad hoc committee put out the call for an Initial Rally, not even one of the strongest wind storms in the history of the country could keep leaders from coming. There were 115 kph winds that snapped ship moorings and brought warnings about the use of exposed roads, but 70 delegates — 20 more than expected — drove and flew in from all over the country.

"This windstorm is evidence of Satan's desire to destroy this movement before it gets started," quipped some of the non-Pentecostal leaders who came.

"No, this is the wind of the Spirit blessing our attempt

188

to disciple our nation," the Pentecostal leaders joked in response.

Faced with data that showed the Church growing at only 1.14 percent AAGR and having only 6.4 percent of the population attending a protestant church, the delegates were stunned. On the other hand, they learned that some denominations were growing as much as 10, 18 and 21 percent a year in a society that was going through unprecedented trauma. The evidences that it might truly be harvest time became clear. The result was that these Church leaders with just about unanimous agreement concluded the time was ripe to launch a major nationwide project.

At the end of the rally, Bruce Patrick of the Baptist Union's Home Mission board of directors seemed to speak for all when he said, "Now is the time for us to band together in a determined effort to reach our whole nation."

The ad hoc committee that called this Initial Rally was quick to seize the opportunity as they guided the delegates into forming an official Executive Committee that would carry the project forward. A strong committee representative of the major blocks of evangelicals was voted in, with the above quoted Bruce Patrick named as chairman.

The Initial Rally that had been so carefully planned and prayed over accomplished its purpose. The ad hoc committee had done its work and was disbanded. The DAWN vision had been "owned," and a structure developed to take it on to the next step.

6. CHOOSE THE NATIONAL COMMITTEE AND THE JOHN KNOXER.

The National Committee in the New Zealand case was elected at the Initial Rally but this is not the only approach. In Ghana, for example, they used the already existing Evangelism Committee of the Ghana Evangelical Fellowship. The Japan Evangelical Fellowship is currently considering the possibility of a DAWN project. If they decide to go ahead, they themselves will select committee members. In the Philippines, the Philippine Council of Evangelical Churches eventually became the official sponsoring body.

In any case, the committee must be composed of men and women who truly own the vision and the goal and who are real workers. The committee must include key representatives from the major denominations and parachurch organizations and from the major blocks of the evangelical Church in a nation. Anyone who looks at the committee should be able to identify with at least someone who represents the same background.

The primary responsibility of this National Committee is to put on a Discipling A Whole Nation (DAWN) Congress. They are now the owners and the policy makers of the project. Theirs is the responsibility of so contextualizing the project that it will really work in their country. They can look to Dawn Ministries as well as the John Knox organization of their country for help, counsel and advice. But it is their project to develop and implement. To them falls the task of discipling their nation, and only when they accept full responsibility for this task will they make the commitment necessary to fulfill it.

Choosing a name

One of the first tasks of the National Committee is to select a name for their DAWN-type project. The word "DAWN" can be used as in the Philippines where they call the project DAWN 2000. In Guatemala they simply used the Spanish work for "dawn" and called it "Amanecer." There was no carry-over of the Disciple A Whole Nation acronym, but that made no difference.

The El Salvador Committee calls their project "Despertar," Spanish for "awakening." "Vision 2000 Canada" and "DAWN Strategy New Zealand" identify the projects in two other countries.

Selecting the executive director

A second and most crucial task of the National Committee will be to select an executive director or national coordinator for the work of the Congress. They need a person with all the qualifications we have ascribed to a John Knoxer with an organization to back him up. Assuming the committee chooses such an individual, he in effect becomes the John Knoxer.

The executive director/John Knoxer is responsible for carrying out the policies of the National Committee. This person reports to the National Committee as the policy-making body, but the buck stops with him. It is up to the executive director to see that everything comes together for an effective DAWN Congress and project. His primary task is to work with each of the Congress committees that are selected by the National Committee.

These usually include the following:

> Finance Committee
> Program Committee
> Facilities Committee
> Invitations Committee
> Research and Book (prophetic message) Committee
> Promotion and Publicity Committee
> Prayer Committee
> Other committees as needed.

7. RAISE THE FINANCES.

Naturally, the National Committee as well as the Finance Committee will have to deal with the ever-present burden of fund raising. Actually, as major nation-wide projects go, DAWN is relatively inexpensive and simple to finance. When the cost per new convert added to the Church through a DAWN project is determined, it will be seen that this approach represents good stewardship.

Financing the Congress itself, according to our experience, is definitely not out of reach of the National Com-

191

mittee.

For one thing, it is the top three to five or ten denominational and parachurch leaders from each group who are being invited to the Congress. Such men and women have access to organizational funds. While it might be quite difficult if not impossible for a village pastor to raise $50 or $100 to attend a conference, it is not out of reach for those who serve in Church headquarters, pastor major city churches or head a parachurch organization.

The nature of the project also seems to appeal to both national and international parachurch organizations that are in a position to help with financing. In several cases the field teams of such organizations have donated their whole evangelism budgets for a year to help the project.

Since the very calling of the John Knox organization is mobilizing the Church of a nation for the discipling of that nation, it will certainly take initiative in helping fund the project either through its own resources or the contacts it has with like-minded groups. Of course, this organization provides much of the funding "in kind" as it channels its personnel, office equipment, and other resources into the project.

This same organization can also be responsible for financing many of the activities that come after the Congress.

At any rate, the cost of the Congress should be kept within the limits of the National Committee's ability to see the funds raised. It will determine how many delegates will come, how much each one will be subsidized, how plush the Congress facilities and lavish the food will be, how expensive the book on the prophetic message will be and the extent of their ability to raise money from within the country and from abroad.

If the DAWN idea is to continue to expand as a movement, it will have to be continuously reproducible from country to country. This calls for a DAWN Congress to be held within the means and abilities of each country that attempts it.

8. HOLD THE CONGRESS.

By the time two to four and up to 12 or 15 leaders representing virtually every evangelical organization in the country gather for a DAWN Congress, there is electricity in the air. These 200 to 400 evangelicals are perhaps fellowshiping together for the first time. It most certainly is the first time such a group has gathered to consider a proven strategy for the discipling of their nation and all its people groups. These leaders have in their power at this moment the ability to mobilize virtually the whole body of Christ in the country.

Sometimes it's more than electricity. After we claimed God's protection and power in a prayer meeting hours before the DAWN Congress started in Guatemala, for example, one leader claims to have had a vision. He was not in the prayer group and did not know the nature of our prayer. He reported, however, seeing an angel with outstretched arms hovering over the swimming pool at the hotel where the conference was about to begin.

At the Congress, this dynamic group will spend two to four days in prayer and Bible study concerning the evangelization of their land. In several sessions they will be taught some of the basic church growth principles. In still more hours, they will be confronted with the data that has been gathered about the Church and the nation.

Then they will be given opportunity to set or ratify a specific goal for filling their land with cells of believers incarnating our risen Lord. In some cases, as in New Zealand, the national goal is determined by adding together all the denominational goals set at the Congress. Conservative estimates of the growth of those not participating are added to this figure to get the final total. In other situations, the research and prophetic message already developed embodies the goal that the whole Congress can agree upon.

One way the setting of this goal has been dramatized is to write out the commitment and goal on a large parchment and then have every delegate who so desires to line up and sign the document.

Whether it comes before or after setting the national goal or goals, each denominational group is given two or more hours to meet in their separate delegations. Here they agree on tentative goals for their particular group. I say tentative, because it will now be necessary to go back to their full organizations and get ownership for the goal and program to reach it. This is a process similar to the national DAWN mechanism.

As we earlier quoted Virgilio Zapata in Guatemala as saying, we leave the Congress ". . . marching under our own flags. But the key is that we go from here marching together" for the discipling of our nation.

9. CONTINUE BEYOND THE CONGRESS.

Unlike other cooperative evangelical efforts, the real work of the DAWN project begins after the main public event is over. The Congress is not the evangelistic activity, merely the situation where the work to be done is decided upon. Now the Church of a country knows what its goals are in terms of churches to be planted and, in some cases, the percent of the population it is to become.

This post-congress work flows along two primary channels. One is the work of each individual denomination, parachurch structure and local church as described in chapter 12. The weeks and months following the Congress are the time for each denomination to begin implementing the "13 Steps to a Successful Growth Program" as presented in Appendix I. It is also the time for mission societies, Bible schools, seminaries and other parachurch organizations to begin modifying and strengthening their programs to work alongside the Church in the multiplication of local congregations. And it is time for each local church to get behind its denominational program and start planting those M1, M2 and M3 daughter churches.

The second channel is the continuing work of the

National Committee and the John Knox organization. Though he carried it out in one region of his country and not at the national level, the work of Jun Balayo in the Philippines provides an excellent model.

After the DAWN Congress in 1980, he went back to the island of Mindanao, which comprises 11 of the provinces of the Philippines, and began developing a regional follow-up program. Over a period of time, he built up a team of full-time workers that was augmented by a number of church growth specialists periodically on loan from other organizations.

This team did continuing research which included an annual study of the growth programs of each denomination and many local churches, a determination of the rate of growth each year for the whole region, examples of successful methodologies and the gathering of all kinds of other data necessary for a DAWN project. Ultimately, they began making an actual list of every barrio without an evangelical church.

This information was published quarterly in a tabloid-size newspaper. Using a large, bold format, it carried well-written reports of the things they were finding through the continuing research. It used pictures, graphs and charts to bring the message home. This publication alone had a key role in keeping the DAWN vision alive, not only in Mindanao but in the rest of the nation as well.

But that wasn't the extent of the work of this effective team. They divided the 11 provinces of Mindanao into about 35 sections with the idea of holding follow-up seminars in every one within a three-year period. This was completed and a second round begun. Now they are returning to each section again with the actual data concerning the barrios still without churches. At these seminars, participants are taking responsibility for planting a church in each of the unchurched barrios on the list.

Another very profitable activity of Balayo and his staff was consulting with denominational leaders. Often such leaders need this kind of boost before they really understand how they should proceed.

In time, a DAWN 2000 Steering Committee was formed just for the Mindanao region. When this committee began to realize the tremendous effectiveness of the follow-up work carried out by Balayo and his team, they reevaluated their share of the goal of 50,000 churches in the country.

The original goal for Mindanao was 11,000 new churches. This would give them one for every 1,000 people. This figure also represented 22 percent of the national goal, corresponding to the percent of population that lived in Mindanao.

By 1988, however, they had an actual count of 9,031 evangelical churches and an estimate of about 2,000 more. They had already reached their AD 2000 goal! With this good news, they revised their goal to 25,000, or 50 percent of the goal for the whole nation!

When the National Committee and John Knox organization follow a pattern something like that of Jun Balayo and his team in Mindanao, a DAWN movement is truly under way in a nation. The discipling of that nation is proceeding at top speed.

This is now happening in the Philippines (as well as other nations). For as the years rolled by there, others began to take more leadership on the national level and are now catching up to Balayo's work in Mindanao. After the goal of 50,000 was first set in 1974, the first actual DAWN 2000 Congress was held in 1980. This was followed by the second in 1985 and the third in 1988. These follow-up congresses have proven so successful in keeping the vision fresh and enrolling new leaders and denominations that they now plan to hold a congress every three years. Fresh data is gathered for these congresses so that an evaluation can be made of progress to date and adjustments necessary for continued or renewed growth.

That covers the story — almost!

As I indicated at the beginning of this chapter, much

more could be, and is being, written about every aspect of how to put on a DAWN Congress and project. The purpose of this chapter was simply to put together in chronological order the materials in previous chapters. By writing Dawn Ministries, the reader can receive further information about developing a DAWN project for his or her country. Additional materials will be sent, correspondence begun and an eventual personal visit made.

For now, that pretty much covers the story of why we need 7 million more churches and how the DAWN strategy can be used as one catalyst to bring them into being.

Oh, one other thing — probably the most important of all. What about the spiritual dynamic necessary for DAWN projects and world evangelization?

My comments on that in the final chapter.

Chapter 16

An Unanswered Prayer

I was a little chagrined by what I was sending Donald McGavran from Manila toward the end of 1966.

Having studied under him at the original Institute of Church Growth in Eugene, Oregon, I had returned to the Philippines to put into practice that which I had learned.

There were all these fantastic principles of how to speed the disciple-making process: research, charts and graphs, goal setting, responsiveness, understanding the complex mosaic of peoples in a country and how to reach them — and a host of other things.

Now I had completed a study of one of the fastest growing denominations in the Philippines — the Four-square Church — and was sending him my first report to be included in a coming issue of the *Church Growth Bulletin*.

In the article I alluded to some of these aspects of church growth, but the main thrust was on the spiritual dynamic of the movement. In conclusion, I wrote this:

> At the bottom of [their tremendous growth] is a
> spiritual dynamic that has driven the Church
> forward. Whatever disagreement there may be
> among other evangelicals concerning how, when
> and by what sign a person is filled with the
> Spirit, there is abundant evidence that a great
> number of Foursquare Church converts in the
> Philippines *are* filled with the Holy Spirit.
> This has resulted in a miraculous ministry that
> frequently parallels the fantastic events recorded
> in the book of Acts. . . .
>
> The greatest need of the Philippines is for
> urgent, sustained prayer for revival that the
> Church might awake to her opportunity — while
> the opportunity is there.[1]

Here I was, a newly trained church growth specialist
writing a report on his first church growth study. *And all I
could write about was the spiritual dynamic that lay
behind this very rapidly growing denomination!*

Donald McGavran hesitated not at all in publishing
the article beginning on the first page of the little magazine. For the truth is, church growth thinking never was
based purely on numbers, pragmatism and mechanical
methodology.

A new wave of the Spirit

Nor do I pin my hopes for the discipling of the nations
and reaching a goal of 5 to 7 million new churches by AD
2000 purely on mechanical implementation of the "how to"
steps expressed in this book. In attempting to obey the final
and great command of our risen Lord, we engage the enemy
in a mortal struggle. What the Lord wants *most* to happen,
Satan wants *least* to happen.

Only with highly developed skills of spiritual warfare will we be able to make significant progress in planting
7 million more churches and in completing the Great Com-

mission. Fortunately, there is a growing awareness of the power of the Holy Spirit available to us in the task of world evangelization.

In his new book, *The Third Wave of the Holy Spirit*,[2] Peter Wagner traces the working of the Holy Spirit in the Pentecostal movement, the charismatic movement and now increasingly in traditional evangelical churches.

He points out the work of David Barrett who estimates the first two waves of the Spirit "numbered 247 million as of 1987 and the third wave 27 million."[3] That is 274 million, a majority of all born-again believers in the world. Those involved in the various movements of the Spirit are the ones showing us how to grow at a rate fast enough to complete the Great Commission in our generation.

From 1950 to 1985, for instance, Pentecostals alone grew from 10 million to 240 million according to Wagner.[4] This gives them an average annual growth rate of 9.5 percent over a 35-year period, a rate almost high enough to provide our 7 million new churches if all denominations were to grow that fast. Since their believers make up the bulk of all evangelicals, the goal of 7 million seems all the closer.

One quite interesting prospect Wagner brings up could further hasten the discipling of nations by filling them with cells of believers.

> Could it be possible [Wagner writes] that Satan, frequently referred to in Scripture as "the god of this age," assigns certain of the demonic spirits under him to promote the kingdom of darkness in given nations, cities, regions, cultural groups, or other segments of the world's population?
>
> If the answer to this question is yes, it becomes obvious that it has tremendous implications for evangelism. If these ruling spirits can be identified and if their power can be broken through spiritual warfare on a high level, the preaching of the gospel of salvation will presumably have freer access to the hearts of those

who are lost. The Apostle Paul speaks of those who are perishing "with minds the god of this age has blinded, who do not believe, lest the light of the gospel of the glory of Christ, who is the image of God, should shine on them" (2 Cor. 4:4). Apparently, one of the major objectives of the devil and his forces of evil is to blind people's eyes so they will not receive the gospel. But if somehow that power can be broken, blind eyes might then see the gospel and allow Jesus Christ to take possession of their lives.[5]

Wagner goes on to cite examples of breaking this power of Satan over cities in Argentina. The resultant turnings to Christ are almost unprecedented in the history of the Church.

The Wheaton revival

The above comments and quotes related to the needed spiritual dynamic are not made lightly, nor are they a tip of the hat to critics of strategies and methodologies. They come out of a lifetime of experience and conviction.

There was the lonely night spent in my dorm room in the winter of 1950, for example.

It was spiritual emphasis week at Wheaton College, and Ed Johnson of Seattle, Washington, was the speaker. Professors were supposed to lighten up on homework so we could all attend the morning and evening sessions.

I suppose my Greek professor *did* ease up, but not to my way of thinking. So I stayed in my room, boning up for class the next day.

By 9:00 p.m. I expected to hear signs of students returning to the dorm. Nothing. I looked at my watch again about 9:30, and felt uneasy because my roommate, Ron Goodman, still had not arrived.

More minutes passed and I grew weary. I went to bed around ten, with still no evidence the meeting was over. *Something special is happening*, I reasoned before dropping off to sleep.

Indeed it was.

In the process of leading songs, Bud Schaeffer — who later became a colleague in Overseas Crusades — asked for a few testimonies. Several were given, but more people kept standing to give theirs. Finally, it was suggested that all who wanted to give a testimony stand and no others would be given such opportunity.

So many stood, however, that they were asked to come forward and occupy the choir loft behind the pulpit. This was soon filled with about 75 students, and long lines began to form.

The dominant theme in these testimonies was confession of sin: of cheating in class, of putting down younger brothers and sisters, of wearing glasses to chapel in order to better see the girls on the other side of the balcony and a host of things more serious.

Nor was it limited to students. My Greek professor (who needed to confess that he had given too much homework that night!) told of the defeat in his life. He had been called to the mission field but turned around on his way to the Philippines. (He later had an excellent missionary career in that land before going to be with the Lord a few years ago.)

Hearing what was going on, I sauntered over to the chapel the next morning. The place was still packed, and one student and professor after another was confessing sin. At first I thought it rather odd, and felt no part of it. But in time, conviction came to my heart as well, and I, too, awaited my turn in the choir loft.

The meeting went on all that day, all that night and the next day and night. It wasn't until word got out of what was happening and TV camera crews from Chicago began turning this sacred time into a media event that a halt was called.

This was the great Wheaton revival of 1950. Though this school got most of the publicity, J. Edwin Orr, the great scholar on revivals, noted there were another 20 or so

203

Christian schools that experienced the same outpouring during that time.

It was here I learned that revival began and was characterized by confession of sin and cleansing of the soul. In the end, it turned out to be a joyous and triumphant experience. But in the process, it was gut-wrenching as the Lord opened our eyes to our ugly sinfulness.

The impression the Wheaton revival made on my life was profound and would never leave me. Never again could I be satisfied with anything less than the outpouring of God's Spirit upon his Church. There would be nothing we could do in our own efforts that could match what God wanted to accomplish through us.

Fire in the Philippines

That, in part, is why I was so open to see the spiritual dynamic of the Foursquare Church in the Philippines many years later. At the heart of their exploding growth was this inner dynamic, the power of the Spirit flowing mightily through them.

By poring over my careful notes taken in interviews with more than 200 of their converts, an incredible picture emerged.

There was the frail, soft-spoken little widow, for example, who worked her way through Bible school by selling vegetables in the market beginning at 2:00 a.m. each day. Within a few years after graduation, she had planted 11 churches with 514 newly converted members.

Signs and wonders followed her ministry after she was converted and healed the same night, filled with the Spirit some months later and eventually graduated from Bible school.

Another interview was with a young, single girl who had passed by an outdoor evangelistic crusade night after night on her way to evening classes in Manila. One night she stopped to listen. The preacher was talking about the healing power of Jesus Christ.

"This is all fakery," she thought. To prove it, she fastened her eyes on a nearby woman with a huge goiter when the evangelist began to pray for the sick in the audience. When the goiter disappeared, she was convinced. She trusted Christ that night and went on to become a powerful Christian worker.

There were scores of such testimonies from the 200 converts I had interviewed.

I had also listened to testimony after testimony of being filled with the Spirit. When I asked these converts what difference this experience made in their lives, I was overwhelmed with their humble and sincere answers. They told of being much bolder in witness, having a greater desire to study the Bible and understanding it better when they did, getting rid of evil habits and sinful practices, loving people much more, having a greater sense of joy and victory in the Christian walk and so on.

Furthermore, I could demonstrate statistically that those who experienced such a filling actually led many more people to Christ than those who did not.

My "hill of faith"

So impressed was I by the genuine and very powerful Christianity I was seeing that I determined to experience it for myself.

Thus I began spending every Sunday afternoon on what I thought of as my "hill of faith." For one thing, this trysting place was in the hills outside Manila where Faith Academy, a school for missionary kids, was located. The other reason for this appellation came through the scripture the Lord led me to after my experience.

After a year of studying the Word and praying there each Sunday afternoon, I felt the presence of the Spirit in a way I was not familiar with. I became lost in prayer. Upon looking at my watch, I realized an hour had passed.

Hoping to get some biblical confirmation of what I was experiencing, I reached for my Bible. The pages fell open to

2 Peter 1:1 where I was struck with these words: "To those who have obtained a faith of equal standing with ours. . . ."

Up to this time, I had thought the meaning of this passage was that we have in effect the same *statement* of faith as the early followers of Christ. While there is truth in that, what I now understood this passage to mean was that we had the *same kind* of faith as those we read about in the Bible.

The faith that closed the mouths of lions, provided food for widows, opened passages through the sea, defeated enemies of the Lord and cooled the fiery furnace was the same kind of faith that had been given to me.

I didn't try to attach a label or find a theological term that would categorize my experience. But I did come to the firm conviction that I was now anointed for the tasks that lay ahead.

Out of that experience came the Christ the Only Way Movement which gave way to the DAWN 2000 project in the Philippines which in turn became the model for the DAWN movement spreading throughout the world.

So while much of this book has focused on the biographical, technical and practical aspects of the DAWN strategy for discipling whole nations, it at the same time pleads for a spiritual movement to undergird and empower the strategy. I praise the Lord for revivals springing up here and there. I'm thrilled with the Concerts of Prayer and other prayer movements now under way. I'm more and more aware of the tremendous spiritual battlefield we enter when we embark upon a project to disciple nations. I am convinced that we need a mighty outpouring of the Spirit in order to complete the task of planting 5 to 7 million more churches by AD 2000 and thus working effectively towards the ultimate completion of the Great Commission.

The latter rain

In fact, I believe such an outpouring of the Spirit is coming.

Though it happened almost 40 years ago, I vividly remember the day I was caught in a downpour on my way back from St. Charles High School near Wheaton, Illinois. I was coming back from what we called "contact work" — hanging out with some pagan high school kids in order to gain a hearing for the good news of Jesus Christ. It had been a somewhat discouraging day, and the Young Life club I was running wasn't doing all that well.

Then came the rainstorm, a deluge, really. The rain washed so hard over the windshield that the wiper could not keep up. I had to pull over to the side of the road to wait it out.

With nothing else to do, why not pray? I pled for the kids, for the club, for the high school.

"Lord, pour out your blessing on this ministry the way you are pouring out your rain over this city," I prayed.

He didn't answer.

At least not right away. A few kids came to trust Christ and we had some successful club meetings. But nothing happened that matched the intensity of my prayer or the enormity of the rain that day.

Over the years, I've wondered about that prayer. It's just now beginning to make sense. It was a prophetic prayer, a prayer for a lifetime of ministry. It was a petition for all peoples everywhere, an agonizing over all the eternally lost and dying of the world.

At this moment I hear the pitter-patter of raindrops around the world. These are the plans and programs and prayers of a growing number of leaders who can see the completion of the Great Commission by the rapidly approaching end of the century.

Soon, I believe, we will experience the deluge — God pouring out his blessing in a mighty movement of his Church leading to his triumphant return.

Revival comes when needed

In a recent sermon at Lake Avenue Congregational

Church, in Pasadena, California, Pastor Paul Cedar quoted Charles Finney as saying that "Revival should be expected whenever it is needed."

More and more of God's people are seeing the "need" to work at the completion of the Great Commission in our generation. Surely a revival of the power of God flowing through his Church is "needed" to accomplish this awesome task. Should we therefore not "expect" that revival to come?

My good friend and colleague, Peter Wagner, is one who expects such a revival:

> I believe the greatest prayer movement in the history of the church is just around the corner. It will blossom in the decade of the 1990s, releasing unprecedented spiritual dynamics towards completing the Great Commission. It will be a principal factor in implementing many of the bold goals for world evangelization zeroing in on the year 2000.[6]

Five to 7 million more evangelical congregations, we believe, is one of those bold goals the Lord is laying before his Church around the world. While we are thrilled with the many evidences of his people taking a significant share of this goal in local, regional, national and even worldwide programs of evangelism and church multiplication, our greatest hope lies in what the Spirit of God is doing and wants to do in our midst.

The Church has experienced the former rain. It is now time for the latter rain — God mightily stirring up his people in obedience to the command given so long ago and now within our grasp to complete.

Notes

1. James H. Montgomery, "What Should Christian Mission Do Today?" *Global Church Growth*, March 1967, p. 206.
2. C. Peter Wagner, *The Third Wave of the Holy Spirit*, (Ann Arbor, Michigan: Vine Books, 1988).
3. Ibid., p. 13.
4. Ibid., p. 89.
5. Ibid., p. 58.
6. C. Peter Wagner, "Praying for Leaders: An Underrated Power Source for World Evangelism," *World Evangelization*, July/August 1988, pp. 24-27.

13 Steps to a Successful Growth Program

(Adapted from an address by Jim Montgomery to the delegates of the 1985 DAWN 2000 Congress in Baguio City, Philippines.)

At the heart of the DAWN (Discipling A Whole Nation) strategy for saturating countries with evangelical congregations until there is one for every small group of people in every ethnic and cultural setting is the Church denomination. It is the denominational growth programs in the Philippines, for example, that have brought about the doubling of the rate of growth for that whole nation in the past 14 years and have kept them on target for growing from 5,000 churches in 1974 to 50,000 or more by AD 2000.

A study of those denominational programs — and those in other nations as well — reveals at least 13 common denominators that seem to be essential ingredients for *any* successful growth program.

Though addressed to denominations, it is assumed these same 13 factors apply for growth programs in local churches or groups of churches in a regional setting.

Here are the 13 steps to a successful growth program.

<u>Step one</u>. *Dream great dreams, see large visions.*

The first common factor is that growing denominations have a vision larger than themselves. They have a driving concern to see their whole region, their whole country won for Christ. Such a challenging goal as a church in every barrio appeals to them. They want to be part of something bigger than themselves.

"Where there is no vision," the Proverb says, "the people perish" (29:18). The verse reminds me of one denominational leader who said, "We are the largest denomination already. We don't have to grow." The result was very slow growth. And, by the way, they are no longer the largest denomination.

Another denominational leader, on the other hand, had a burning desire to see his whole province filled with churches. The result was hundreds of churches planted and thousands of converts being discipled.

When you dream great dreams and see large visions, you are driven to work persistently toward seeing them accomplished.

<u>Step two</u>. *Develop, maintain and use a solid base of data.*

The Living Bible translates Proverbs 18:13 this way: "What a shame — yes, how stupid! — to decide before knowing the facts!"

The second common denominator in successful growth

programs is that denominations not only have their heads in the clouds but have their feet on the ground. They see that the way to accomplish their dreams is not through sentimental, emotional fantasizing, but through a concrete understanding of their situation.

These denominations study their context to see who is responsive to the gospel and how best to reach the people in it. They study their own resources to see how big they are, how fast they are growing and what their effective and ineffective methods are. They study other growing churches and denominations to find good ideas for their own programs.

I have a whole seminar on this topic, but I think you already have a growing appreciation of the importance of keeping detailed records on each aspect of your Church, of gathering and analyzing that data and of using it to set goals and make plans.

Step three. **Set challenging, realistic and measurable goals.**

This, I believe, is at the heart of effective denominational growth programs. Challenging goals stir up and mobilize the people. Laymen and women get involved to an extent that surprises even themselves. It is exciting to work together toward a worthwhile and challenging goal.

Realistic goals are set so as not to discourage people. If goals are not based on previous experience (the facts) and in terms of what is possible (responsiveness), they can be worse than no goals at all. Goals should be set large enough to be challenging, but realistic enough to avoid discouragement.

Measurable goals are set so the people can rejoice in their achievement. Specific numbers and specific dates get members involved.

I am frequently told that people in non-Western nations do not respond to goals, that they are more relational in orientation. But setting goals works, I believe, because it is biblical and therefore above culture. Goals set under the guidance of the Spirit are "the substance of things hoped for, the evidence of things not seen" (Heb. 11:1).

In other words, goal setting by the Christian is an act of faith, without which "it is impossible to please God" (Heb. 11:5).

Step four. Achieve goal ownership.

In one very large denominational program I am familiar with, the foreign missionaries got together and set their ten-year goal. Then they had a very difficult time getting the Church to work toward it.

In their second program, however, everyone had a say in what the goal should be. They argued and wrestled with each other until everyone was satisfied it was the right goal. Since everyone now "owned" the goal, they all worked hard to achieve it.

This is a very crucial step in a successful growth program, and can be skipped only at great cost.

Step five. Give a name to your program.

The colorful names used in the Philippines give evidence of creative thinking in this area. The best names are not only colorful but also descriptive of what the goal is. "Strategy 1085 by 1985" and "Expansion 100" are good examples.

How would your children feel if they were given no names? Lost, ignored, unimportant! So a program needs strong identity if it is to be supported and completed. Give it a good name.

Step six. Develop a functional organizational structure.

As we see the Church enjoying explosive growth in the book of Acts, we find that many changes had to take place.

One of these is recorded in the sixth chapter. As the Church increased in number, there developed a problem in administration. This was solved by the development of a new layer of leadership and giving a new whole group of laymen more responsibility.

As one denomination after another developed growth programs and actually experienced increased growth in the Philippines, we found that they also had to redesign their organizational structures. Leaders had to be found to oversee the total program, take leadership in a host of committees, oversee prayer programs, supervise the recording and reporting of statistics, develop and produce various publications and handle training programs.

For your growth program to succeed, you will have to break out of some of your traditional organizational structures. In the process, you will also have the joy of seeing many more laymen and women switch from being bench warmers to active participants in the church. And your denomination will grow spiritually and numerically.

Step seven. *Depend on prayer and the power of the Spirit.*

Critics of the type of movement in which you are involved sometimes have the impression that concern for numbers and the wisdom of people are substitutes for the work of the Holy Spirit. My observation is that just the opposite is true. Denominational programs that are truly successful are those that have been solidly backed by prayer.

The Target 400 program of the C.M.A. is a good example. They appointed a national prayer chairman and made her a member of the executive committee. She helped organize hundreds of prayer cells in their churches and kept them supplied with a stream of prayer requests for the movement. The result was thousands more laypeople actually involved in group prayer than they ever had before.

215

The book of Acts certainly models this need for dependence on prayer and the power of the Spirit in relation to the growth of the Church. The 120 spent many days in fasting and prayer before the advent of the Holy Spirit and the first 3,000 converts. Then it was a miracle of healing that led to the conversion of the next 2,000 men.

Acts 16:5 says, "The churches were strengthened in the faith, *and* they increased in numbers daily." Both from the Word of God and the present experience of his Church we must conclude that spiritual dynamic and growth of the church go hand in hand.

Step eight. Keep your members motivated and informed.

In the growth programs I have observed, I have found many creative ideas for keeping people from losing interest. First and foremost is a steady stream of announcements, reports and related sermons from the pulpits of the local churches.

Almost all have found it necessary to put out a regular publication that reports outstanding results, answers to prayer and progress toward goals. Such periodicals include articles on the biblical and practical foundations of the movement and feature men and women who have made outstanding contributions.

Added to these basic tools of communication are a host of other motivators such as annual rallies, special sessions and annual meetings, yearbooks with pictures of each church, seminars, and even such things as printed T-shirts and book markers.

Denominations need to give much thought, planning and prayer to the teaching and activity necessary to keep the program moving forward month after month and year after year. Of course, the greatest motivator of all from a human standpoint is the thrill of actually reaching the goals that have been set.

Step nine. *Train your members.*

This has been an indispensable part of any significant growth program, as might well be expected. The biblical strategy is to equip (train) the saints (laymen and women) *for the work of the ministry.*

In successful denominational programs, members are trained for every aspect of the program. This includes training for starting and pastoring churches, starting and leading evangelistic Bible study groups, leading committees for record keeping and for data gathering and analysis, prayer groups, finances, executive leadership, communications and so on.

Training is given in every type of situation from Bible schools and seminaries, to short term and TEE training programs to informal and apprenticeship programs. Equipping and training are the basic ministry of the Church. No program will reach its goals without effectiveness in this area.

Step ten. *Create sound financial policy.*

Denominations creating strong, new growth programs are forced to evaluate their whole financial structure. For one thing, they need to evaluate just how they are spending their money. Frequently funds can be diverted from lower priority items to the challenging evangelistic thrust before them.

Another matter is developing methodologies for promoting the program, training the workers and starting new churches that are effective yet within the means of local churches and national denominations.

A third matter is effective fund-raising programs. No denomination or church I know of is seeing their members come anywhere near a standard of a tithe of total income. Good teaching and creative planning are needed in this area.

No growth program is going to reach its goals without an overhaul of its finances in these three areas.

Step eleven. *Send out missionaries.*

When the Conservative Baptists in the Philippines saw their annual growth rates fall from above 20 percent in 1974 to 12.1 and 12.8 the next two years, they realized the program was in trouble unless some firm action was taken. Among other things, they sent out missionaries.

Vic Andaya went to the province of Nueva Ecija and saw 84 converts enter his new church the first year. Dave Billings pushed this work out to include Nueva Viscaya and Isabela provinces.

At about the same time, Robert Skivington was developing a thorough plan for a responsive tribe way off in Mindanao. In the first year alone they saw about 400 come to Christ and into new churches.

This missionary thrust reestablished strong momentum for their ongoing program, and is a beautiful example of how local churches and denominations must see beyond their own circumscribed areas for continued growth. Every church needs to be challenging, training and sending out missionaries to neighboring barrios and more distant provinces and peoples. A vast new emphasis on missions, which is actually now developing, is crucial to reaching local, denominational and national goals.

Step twelve. *Regularly evaluate progress.*

The strength of having measurable goals is that it is always possible to see just where you are in relation to those goals. In the illustration just mentioned, the Conservative Baptists might never have developed such a strong missionary emphasis if they had not known they were falling short of their goals. After all, they were still adding new members and new churches at a rather good rate. How would they have known they were slowing down if they had not set a goal and evaluated progress in terms of that goal?

Leaders of each program must constantly be aware of

progress being made toward goals, problems that are arising in any of these 13 steps we are presenting and new opportunities and trends in their community, region and nation.

An annual evaluation with data in hand lasting two or three days is the twelfth essential ingredient in an effective growth program.

Step thirteen. *Make new plans.*

By far, the most heartening aspect of the 50,000 by 2000 movement in the Philippines is the sequence of growth programs. Scarcely is one goal reached and one program successfully completed when another, grander goal is set.

I remind you of the C.M.A. Target 400 program being followed by the Target 100,000 plan which gave way to their Two, Two, Two project: 20,000 churches and 2,000,000 members by the year 2000. Several others could be cited.

In this way, evangelism and church planting become a regular part of the church life rather than an activity engaged in only at long, irregular intervals. In this way, and only in this way, will the goal of 50,000 by 2000 be reached.

Each year as the current project is evaluated, new plans must be made for the coming year, made in light of the evaluation. As each five- or ten-year project nears completion, it too must be evaluated and new plans made based on this evaluation.

The Church of the Philippines will make a great leap ahead in the discipling of its nation and in the cause of world evangelization with this good habit of making and carrying out plans, evaluating progress, and making new plans in light of the current situation.

These, then, are the 13 common denominators I have discovered in successful denominational programs here and abroad. Study them, pray about them and develop your program incorporating these 13 essential steps.

Appendix II

Ordering *DAWN* *Materials*

1. *DAWN Report*

This 16-page quarterly publication keeps the the reader abreast of what is happening in the DAWN movement around the world with news reports, ideas on strategy, new books and materials.

Subscription is free of charge.

2. "The Challenge of a Whole Country"

Of this paper, presented at the 1982 EFMA Missions Consultation, Vergil Gerber said, "This has become an historic conference and you have written a landmark paper that can change the course of missions. . . . You have given us the program [for world evangelization]."

(19 pages, typescript, written by Jim Montgomery)

Price: $1.85 postage paid to U.S. address
$2.20 postage paid to overseas address

3. "Rise and Possess the Land"

For the first time ever, the DAWN strategy has been applied to a county in the United States. Project name is RISE (Research In Strategic Evangelization) Santa Clara County. "Rise and Possess the Land" is the 40-page address given by Jim Montgomery to the Congress held in November 1986. It explains the DAWN concept in light of the Joshua model of possessing the land, and shows how protestant churches in Santa Clara County, California, can triple their average attendance by AD 2000.

It is the basic document for anyone desiring to know how DAWN can be applied to a city, county or state in the U.S.

Price: $3.20 postage paid to U.S. address
    $4.00 postage paid to overseas address

4. *God's Hour for Guatemala*

This is the first book written specifically for the Church of a nation *before* a DAWN Congress and project got under way. Based on careful research, it is the prophetic message to Guatemalan evangelicals on how they can become 50 percent of the population by 1990.

Written by Jim Montgomery with a significant chapter by Emilio Antonio Núñez. 50 pages typescript.

Price: $3.95 postage paid to U.S. address
    $4.90 postage paid to overseas address

La Hora de Dios Para Guatemala is the original book published in Spanish. Includes additional chapters by Núñez and Galo Vasquez.

Price: $3.95 postage paid to U.S. address
    $4.90 postage paid to overseas address

5. DAWN Strategy New Zealand: Initial Findings of a Research Analysis on the People and the Church of New Zealand.

This just-completed 60-page manuscript provides background for the project now under way in the first Western nation to implement DAWN. It demonstrates how societal conditions and a variety of growth rates and factors indicate this is the appointed time to make an effort to disciple the whole nation.

Written by Bob Hall of the Department of Sociology at the University of Canterbury and Wolfgang Fernandez of Dawn Ministries.

Price: $4.95 postage paid to U.S. address
        $5.90 postage paid to overseas address

6. The Church Growth Survey Handbook

Written by Peter Wagner and Bob Waymire, this manual has become a best-seller in missions circles. Its 40 pages provide a step-by-step account of how to measure the growth of churches and therefore make realistic plans for future growth.

Available in English and Spanish!

Price: $4.15 postage paid to U.S. address
        $5.55 postage paid to overseas address

7. DAWN Consultants and Speakers

For those leaders in countries around the world who have caught the DAWN vision and have the organizational structure to develop a DAWN project, Dawn Ministries by arrangement can provide free consulting service in many parts of the world.

Speakers also are available for church services, mission conferences and seminars.

Consultants and speakers bilingual in Spanish and English and French and English are available.

HOW TO ORDER

Any correspondence or orders for materials should be sent to Dawn Ministries, P.O. Box 40969, Pasadena, CA 91114.

Please accompany all orders with checks drawn on U.S. banks only. Our postage-paid prices include inexpensive air forwarding delivery to overseas addresses. We are a nonprofit organization: all items priced at cost.

Be sure to include your name and address clearly *printed.*

Index